For Engineers & Designers

KeyCreator Exercises

200 3D PRACTICE DRAWINGS

SACHIDANAND JHA

Dear Reader,

Thank you for choosing **KeyCreator Exercises** book. This book is part of a family of premium-quality CADIN360 books, all of which are written by Outstanding author who combine practical experience with a gift for teaching.

CADIN360 was founded in 2016. More than 3 years later, we're still committed to producing consistently exceptional books. With each of our titles, we're working hard to set a new standard for the industry. From the paper we print on, to the authors we work with, our goal is to bring you the best books available.

I hope you see all that reflected in these pages. I'd be very interested to hear your comments and get your feedback on how we're doing. Feel free to let me know what you think about this or any other CADIN360 book by sending me an email at contactus@cadin360.com.

If you think you've found a technical error in this book, please visit https://cadin360.com/contact-us/.
Customer feedback is critical to our efforts at CADIN360.

Best regards,

Sachidanand Jha
Founder & CEO, CADIN360

KeyCreator Exercises

Published by
CADIN360
cadin360.com
Copyright © 2019 by CADIN360, All rights reserved.

Limit of Liability/Disclaimer of Warranty:

Examination Copies

Electronic Files

Disclaimer:

Preface

KeyCreator Exercises

❖ This book contain 200 CAD practice exercises and drawings.

❖ This book does not provide step by step tutorial to design 3D models.

❖ S.I Unit is used.

❖ Predominantly used Third Angle Projection.

❖ This book is for **KeyCreator** and Other Feature-Based Modeling Software such as Inventor, SolidWorks, NX, Solid Edge, AutoCAD, PTC Creo etc.

❖ It is intended to provide Drafters, Designers and Engineers with enough 3D CAD exercises for practice on **KeyCreator**.

❖ It includes almost all types of exercises that are necessary to provide, clear, concise and systematic information required on industrial machine part drawings.

❖ Third Angle Projection is intentionally used to familiarize Drafters, Designers and Engineers in Third Angle Projection to meet the expectation of world wide Engineering drawing print.

❖ Clear and well drafted drawing help easy understanding of the design.

❖ This book is for Beginner, Intermediate and Advance CAD users.

❖ These exercises are from Basics to Advance level.

❖ Each exercises can be assigned and designed separately.

❖ No Exercise is a prerequisite for another. All dimensions are in mm.

❖ Note: Assume any missing dimensions.

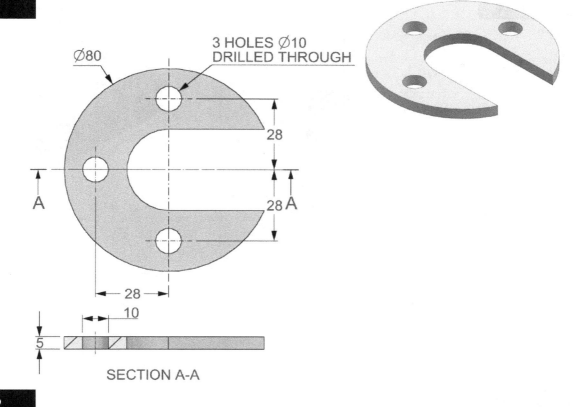

Ø80

3 HOLES Ø10
DRILLED THROUGH

28

28 A

A

28

10

5

SECTION A-A

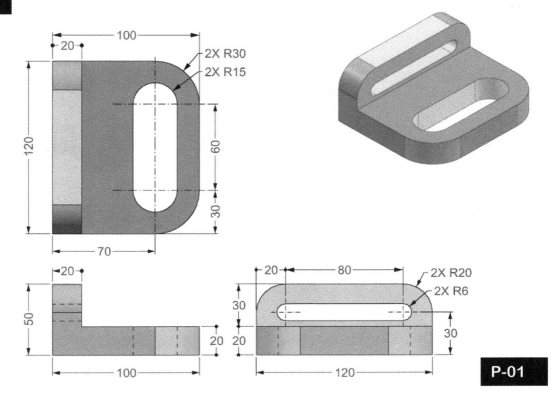

100

20

2X R30
2X R15

120

60

30

70

20

50

20

100

20

30

20 20

80

2X R20
2X R6

30

120

EX-03

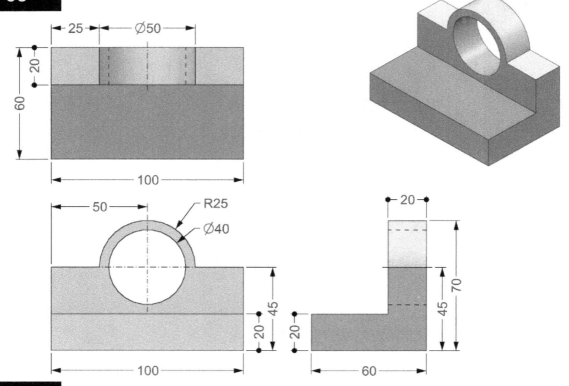

25 Ø50

20

60

100

50 R25
Ø40

45

20 20

100

20

70

45

60

EX-04

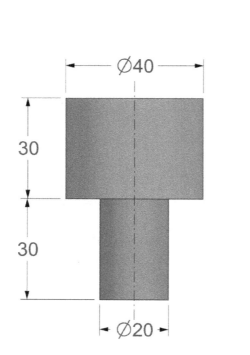

Ø40

30

30

Ø20

P-02

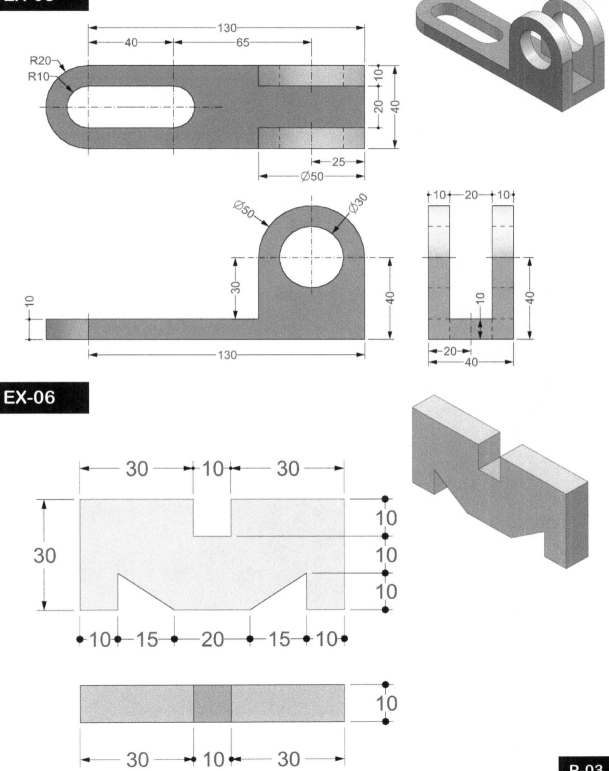

EX-05

EX-06

P-03

EX-07

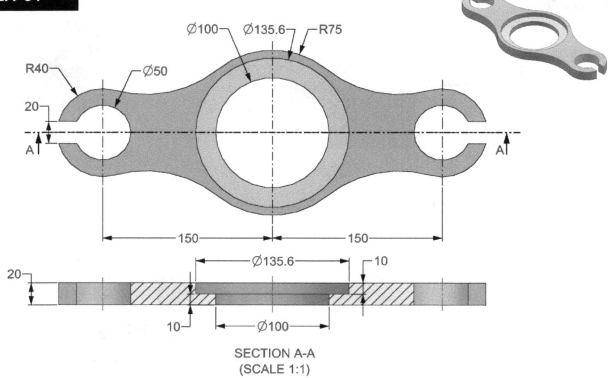

Ø100 Ø135.6 R75
R40 Ø50
20
A
A
150 150

20
Ø135.6 10
10 Ø100

SECTION A-A
(SCALE 1:1)

EX-08

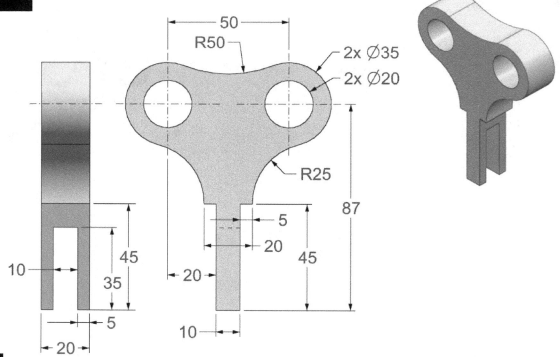

50
R50 2x Ø35
2x Ø20
R25
87
5
20
45
45
10 20
20
10
35
5
20

P-04

EX-09

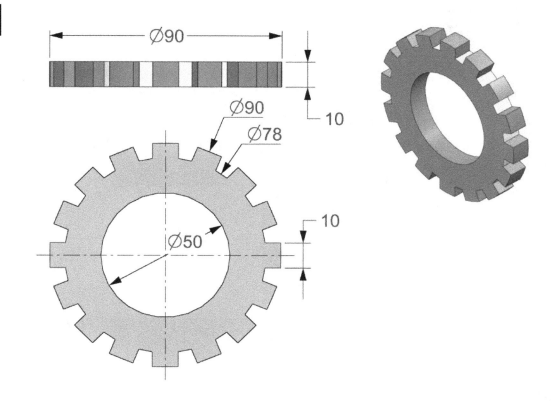

Ø90

10

Ø90
Ø78
Ø50

10

EX-10

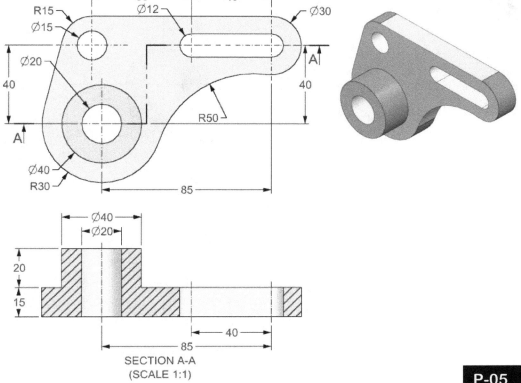

50   40

R15
Ø15   Ø12   Ø30

Ø20

A

40   40

R50

A

Ø40
R30   85

Ø40
Ø20

20

15

40

85

SECTION A-A
(SCALE 1:1)

P-05

EX-11

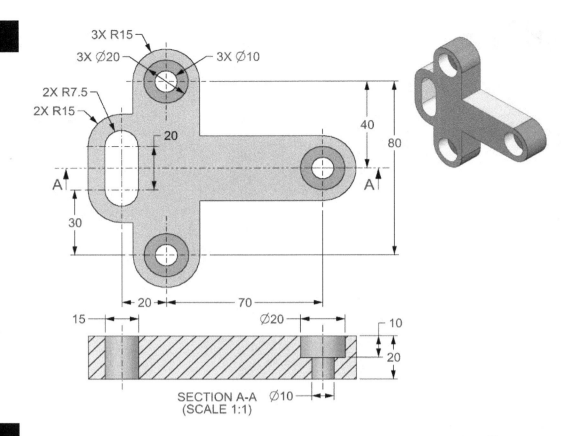

3X R15
3X Ø20
3X Ø10
2X R7.5
2X R15
20
A
40
80
30
A
20
70

15
Ø20
10
20

SECTION A-A
(SCALE 1:1)
Ø10

EX-12

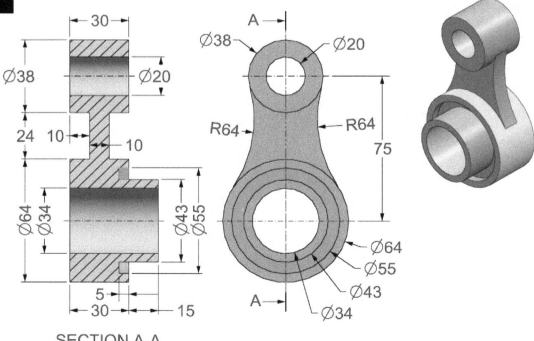

30
Ø38
Ø20
A
Ø38
Ø20
24
10
10
R64
R64
Ø64
Ø34
Ø43
Ø55
75
Ø64
Ø55
5
Ø43
30
15
Ø34
A

SECTION A-A
(SCALE 1:1)

P-06

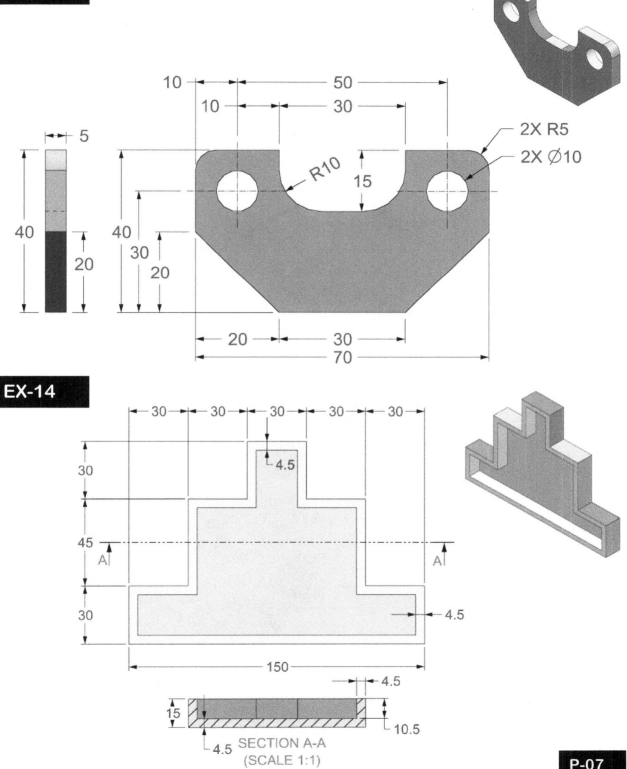

EX-13

10
50
10
30
2X R5
2X Ø10
5
R10
15
40
40
30
20
20
30
70

EX-14

30 30 30 30 30
30
4.5
30
45
A
A
30
4.5
150
4.5
15
10.5
4.5
SECTION A-A
(SCALE 1:1)

P-07

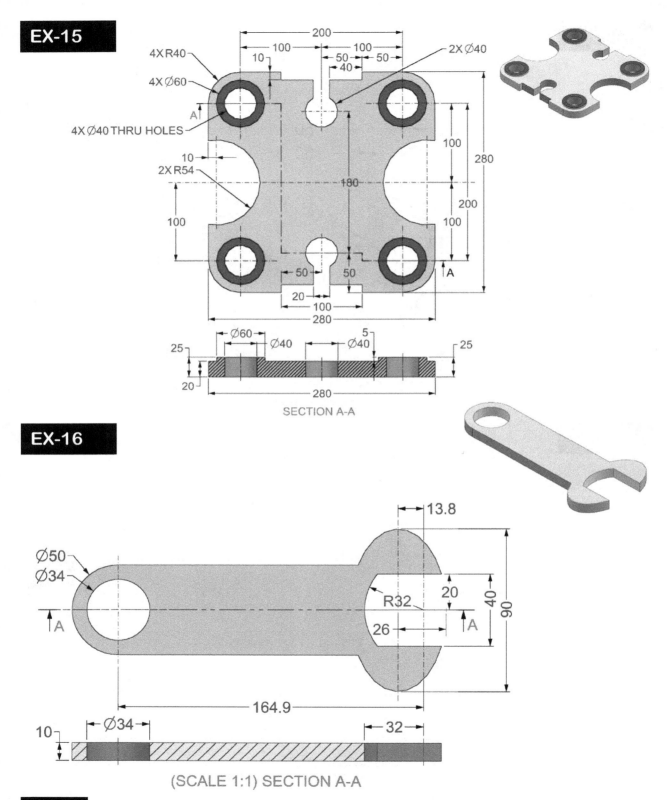

EX-15

4X R40
4X Ø60
4X Ø40 THRU HOLES
2X R54

200
100
10
100
50
50
40
2X Ø40

100
280
100
200
180
100

10

100

50
50
20
100
280

Ø60
Ø40
Ø40
5
25
25
20
280

SECTION A-A

EX-16

Ø50
Ø34

13.8

20
40
90
R32
26

A
A

164.9

10
Ø34
32

(SCALE 1:1) SECTION A-A

P-08

EX-17

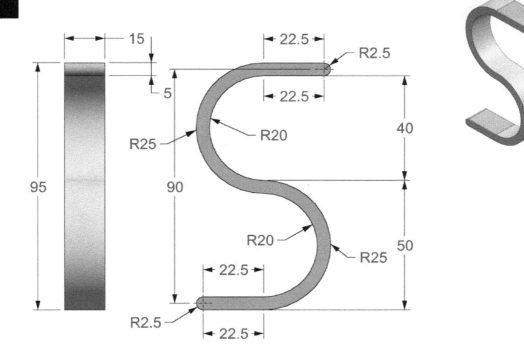

15

22.5

R2.5

22.5

5

R25 R20

40

90

R20

50

R25

95

22.5

R2.5

22.5

EX-18

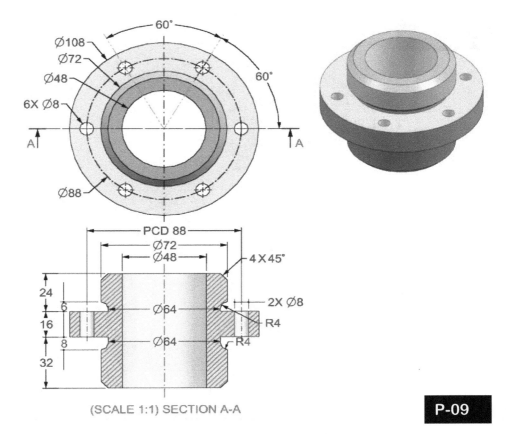

60°

Ø108

Ø72

Ø48

60°

6X Ø8

A

A

Ø88

PCD 88

Ø72

Ø48

4 X 45°

24

6

Ø64

2X Ø8

16

R4

8

Ø64

R4

32

(SCALE 1:1) SECTION A-A

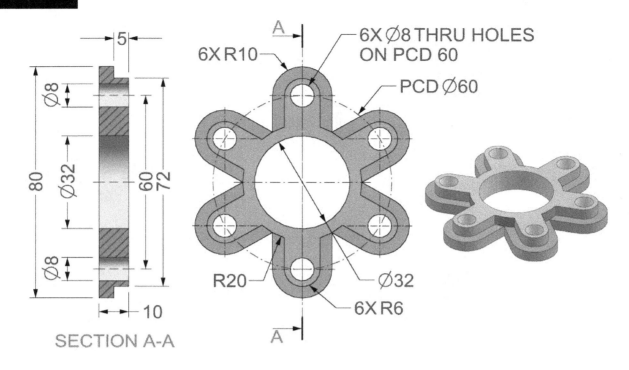

6X R10

6X Ø8 THRU HOLES
ON PCD 60

PCD Ø60

5

Ø8

Ø32

80

60

72

Ø8

10

R20

Ø32

6X R6

SECTION A-A

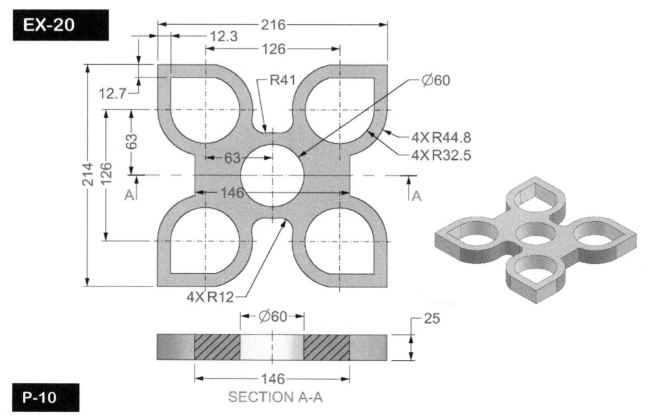

216

12.3

126

12.7

R41

Ø60

63

214

126

63

4X R44.8
4X R32.5

146

A

A

4X R12

Ø60

25

146

SECTION A-A

EX-21

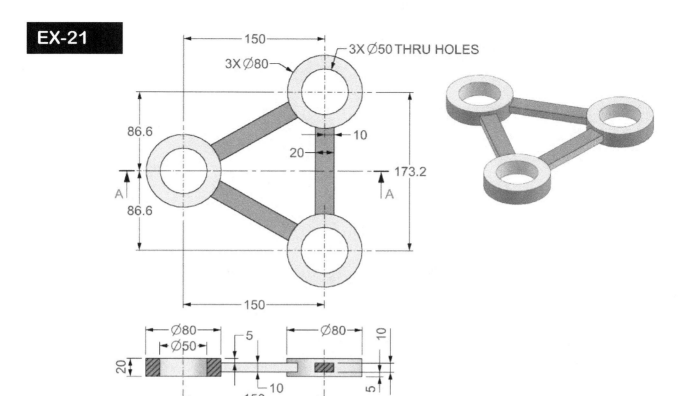

150

3X Ø50 THRU HOLES

3X Ø80

86.6

10

20

173.2

86.6

A

A

150

Ø80

Ø50

5

Ø80

10

20

10

5

150

SECTION A-A

EX-22

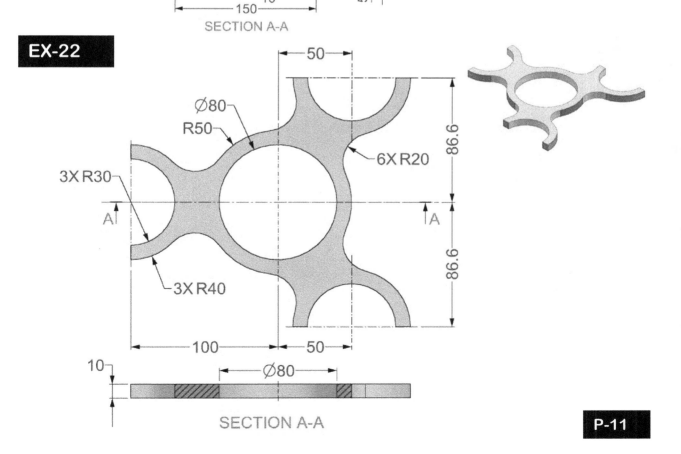

50

Ø80

R50

86.6

6X R20

3X R30

A

A

86.6

3X R40

100

50

10

Ø80

SECTION A-A

P-11

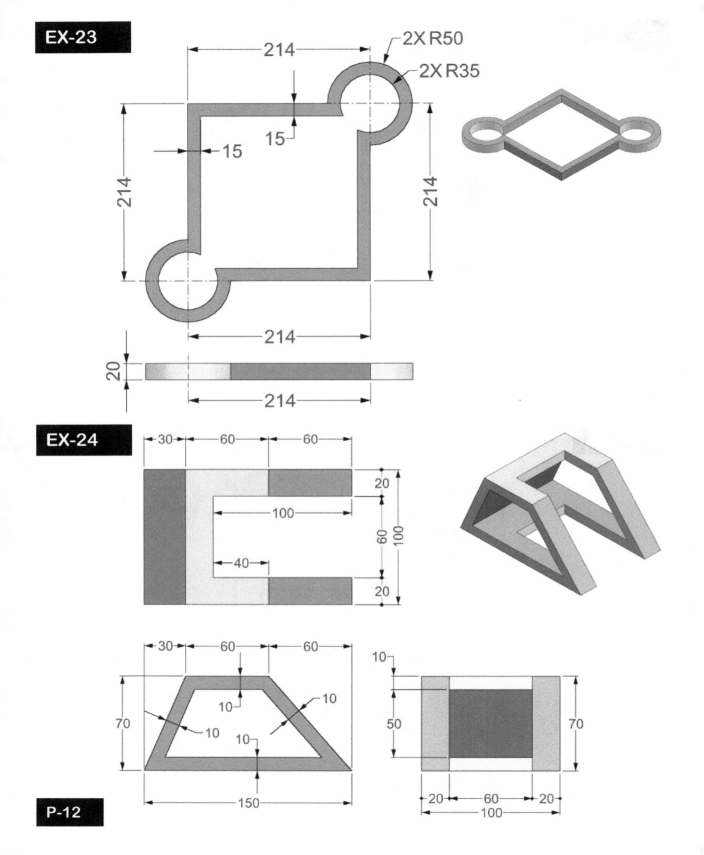

EX-23

214

2X R50

2X R35

15

15

214

214

214

20

214

EX-24

30 · 60 · 60

20

100

60 · 100

40

20

P-12

30 · 60 · 60

10

70

10 · 10

10

150

10

50

70

20 · 60 · 20

100

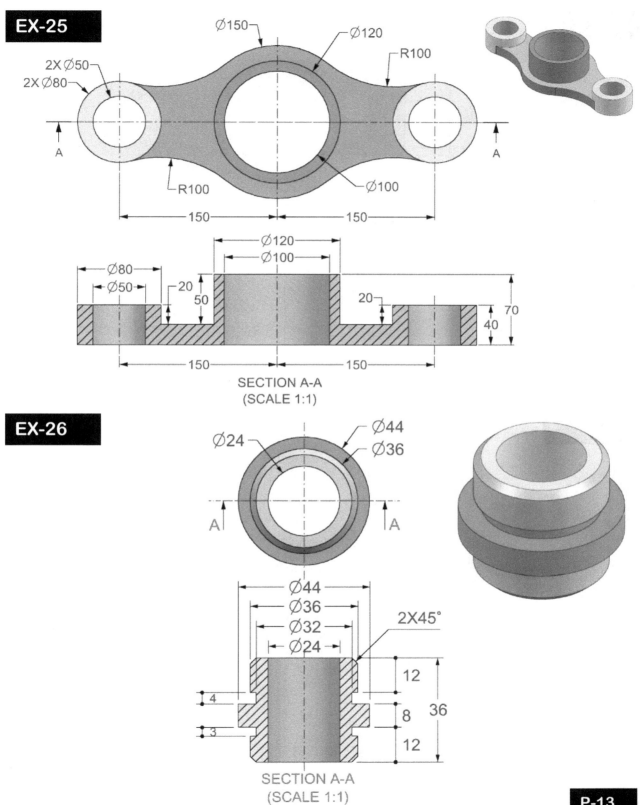

EX-25

Ø150
Ø120
R100
2X Ø50
2X Ø80
A
A
R100
Ø100
150
150

Ø120
Ø100
Ø80
Ø50
20
50
20
70
40
150
150

SECTION A-A
(SCALE 1:1)

EX-26

Ø24
Ø44
Ø36
A
A

Ø44
Ø36
Ø32
Ø24
2X45°
12
4
8
36
3
12

SECTION A-A
(SCALE 1:1)

EX-27

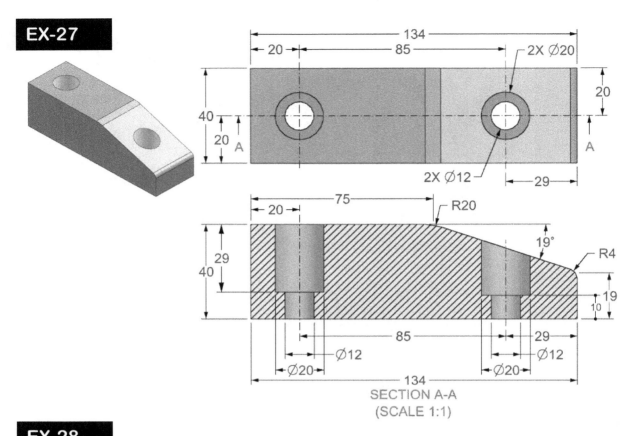

134
20
85
2X ⌀20
20
40
20
A
A
2X ⌀12
29

20
75
R20
19°
R4
29
40
19
10
85
29
⌀12
⌀12
⌀20
⌀20
134

SECTION A-A
(SCALE 1:1)

EX-28

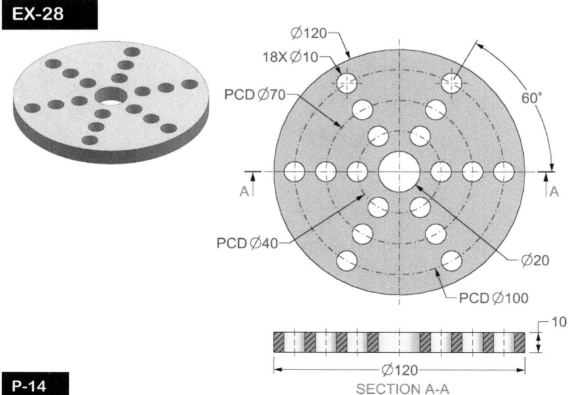

⌀120
18X ⌀10
PCD ⌀70
60°
PCD ⌀40
⌀20
PCD ⌀100
10
⌀120

SECTION A-A

EX-29

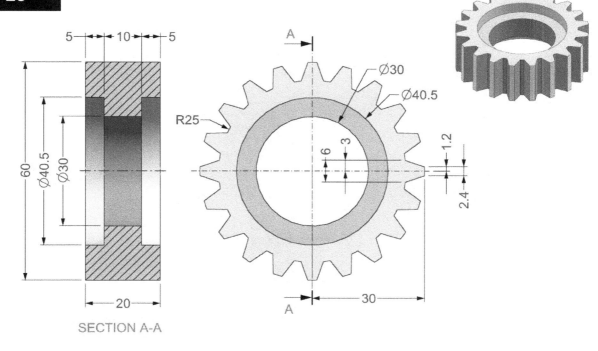

SECTION A-A

EX-30

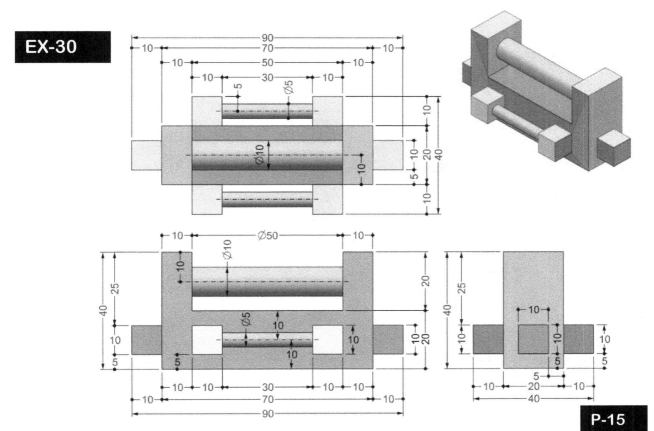

P-15

EX-31

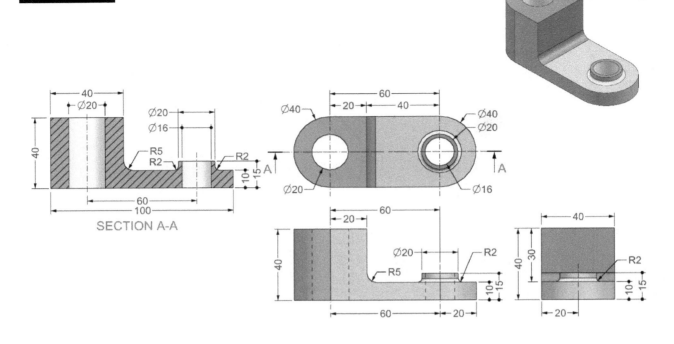

SECTION A-A

EX-32

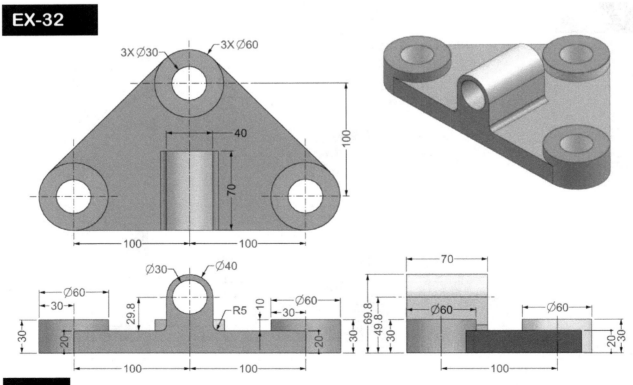

P-16

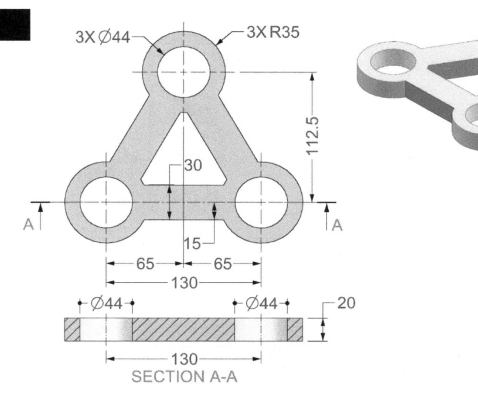

3X Ø44 — 3X R35

112.5

30

15

65 65

130

Ø44 Ø44 — 20

130

SECTION A-A

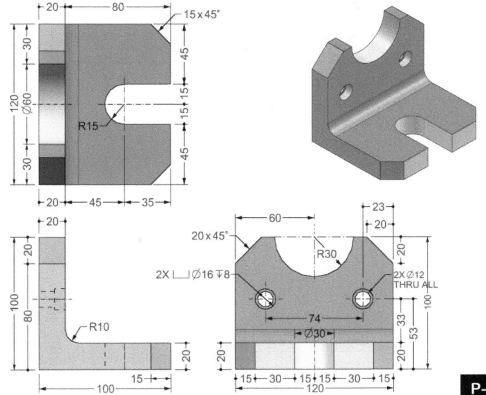

20 80 15 x 45°

30

45

120

Ø60

15 15

R15

15

45

20 45 35

20

20

100

80

R10

20

15

100

60 23

20 x 45° R30 20

2X ⌴ Ø16 ↧8 2X Ø12 THRU ALL

74

Ø30

33

53

20

15 30 15 15 30 15 20

120

100

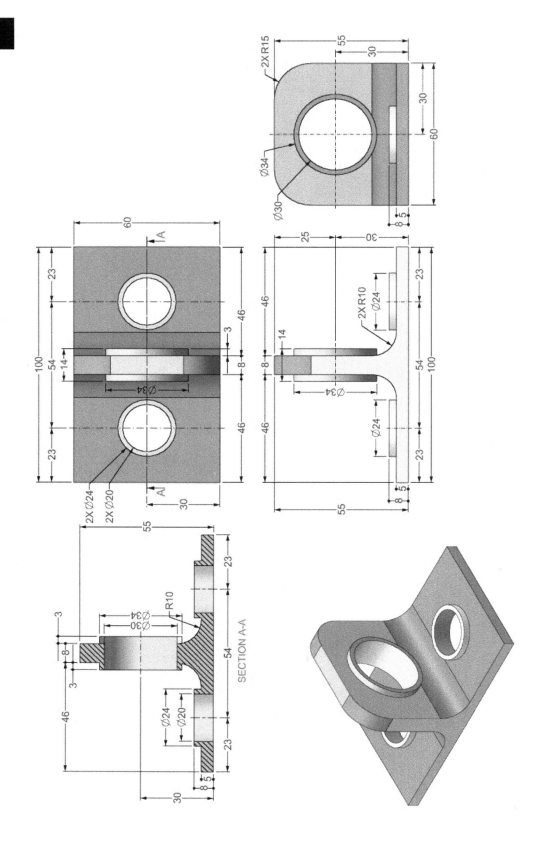

SECTION A-A

EX-36

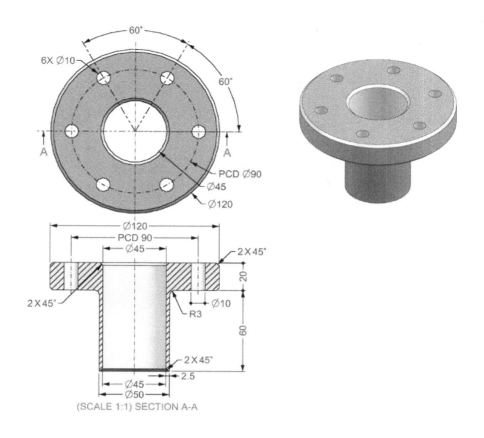

60°
60°
6X Ø10
PCD Ø90
Ø45
Ø120

A — A

Ø120
PCD 90
Ø45
2 X 45°
2 X 45°
Ø10
R3
20
60
2 X 45°
2.5
Ø45
Ø50
(SCALE 1:1) SECTION A-A

EX-37

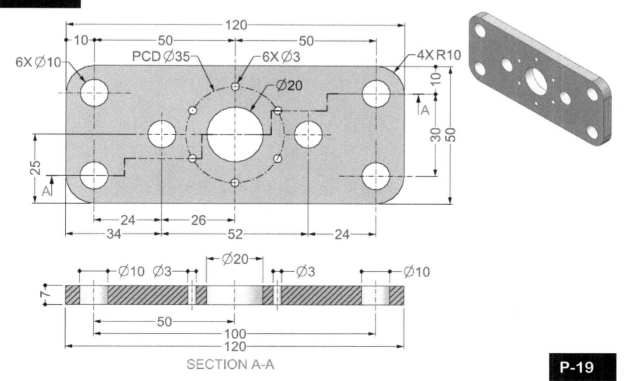

120
10
50
50
6X Ø10
PCD Ø35
6X Ø3
4X R10
Ø20
10
A
30
50
25
A
24
26
34
52
24

Ø20
Ø10 Ø3
Ø3
Ø10
7
50
100
120
SECTION A-A

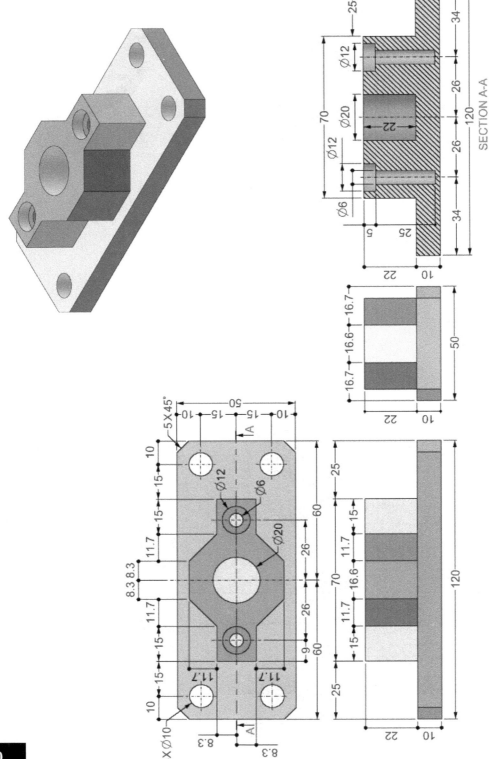

SECTION A-A

EX-39

70

R20
Ø20

40

45

R25
Ø20

45

20

30

10

10

A

A

45

65

2X R10

Ø40

Ø20

20

25

45

SECTION A-A

EX-40

Ø60

20

10

Ø50

5

Ø60
Ø50

5 — 10 — 5

30

Ø60

20

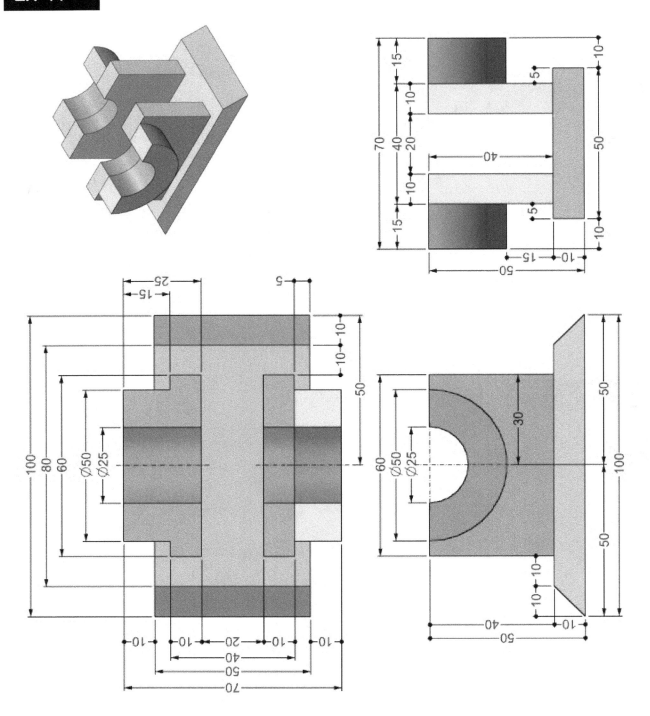

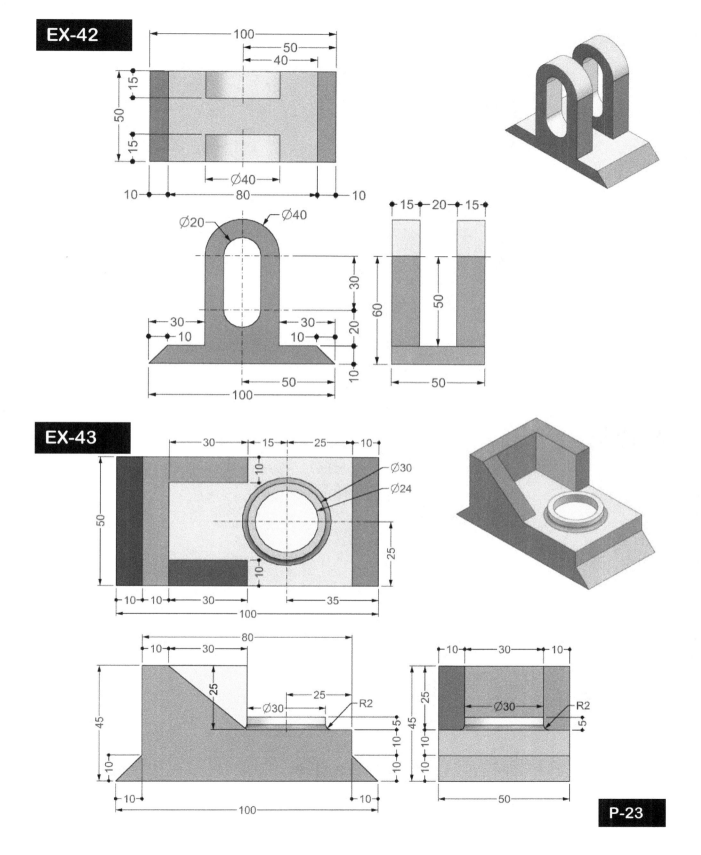

EX-42

100
50
40
15
50
15
Ø40
10 • • 80 • • 10

Ø20 Ø40
30
30 • 30
20
60
10 10
50
100

15 • 20 • 15
50
60

EX-43

30 • 15 • 25 • 10
10
Ø30
Ø24
50
25
10
10 • 10 • 30 • 35
100

80
10 • 30
25
25
Ø30
R2
45
5
10
10
10 10
10 • 10
100

10 • 30 • 10
25
45
Ø30
R2
5
10
10
50

P-23

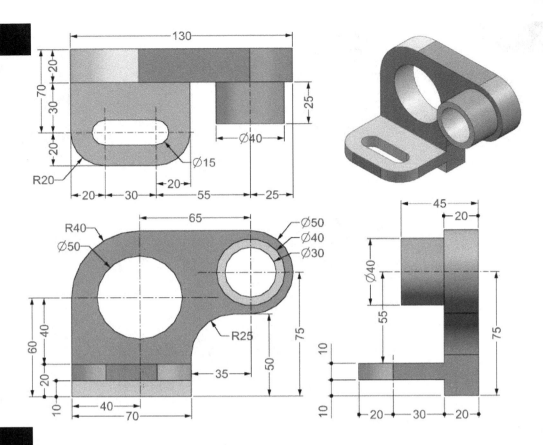

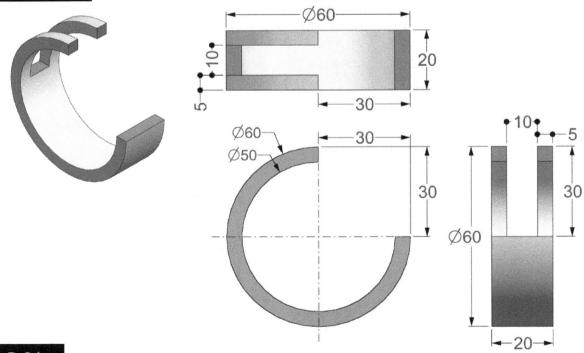

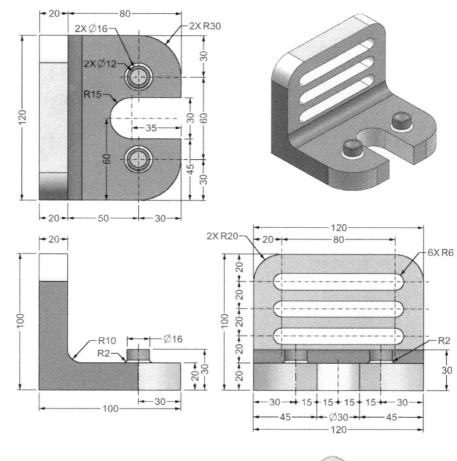

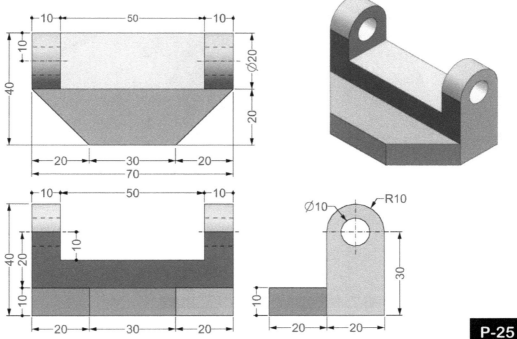

EX-48

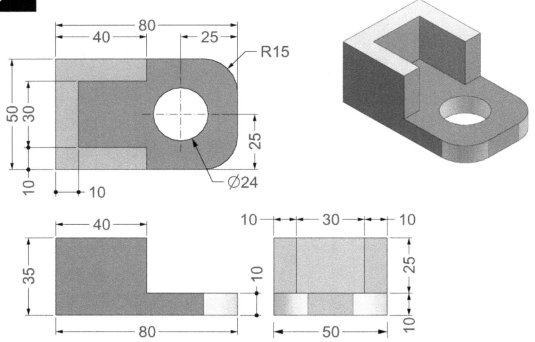

EX-49

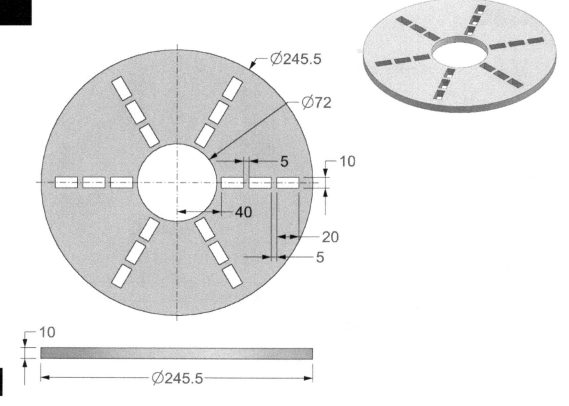

P-26

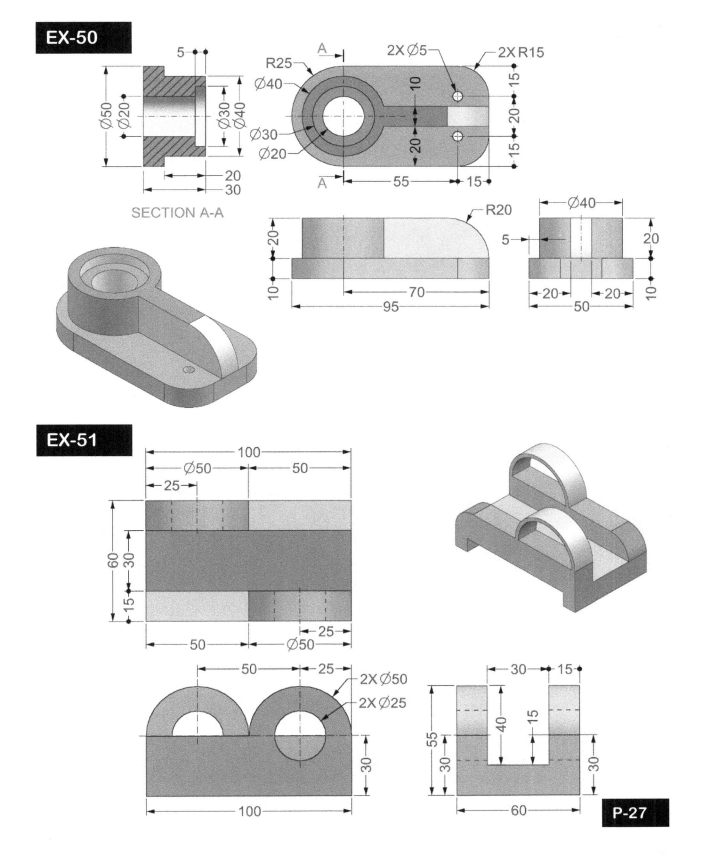

EX-50

5

R25
Ø40
Ø50
Ø20
Ø30
Ø40
Ø30
Ø20

20
30

SECTION A-A

A
2X Ø5
2X R15

10
15
20
15

20

55   15

R20

20
10

70
95

Ø40
5
20

20
50
10

EX-51

100
Ø50   50
25

60
30
15

50
Ø50
25

2X Ø50
2X Ø25

50   25

30

100

30   15

55
40
15
30
30

60

P-27

EX-52

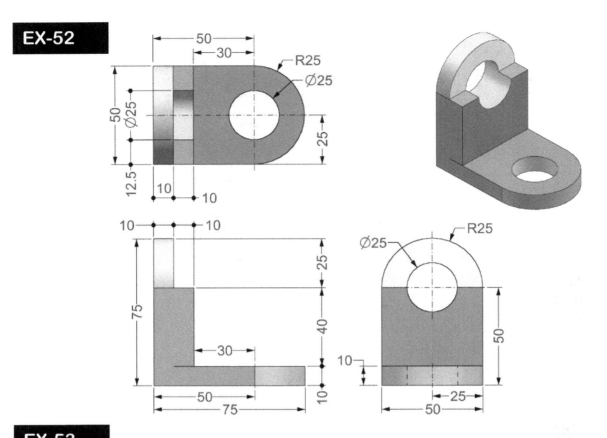

EX-53

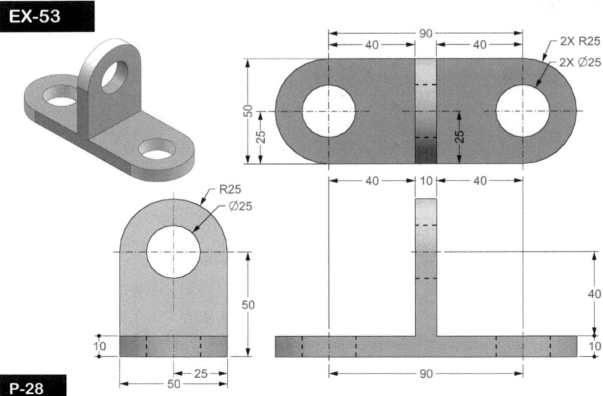

P-28

EX-54

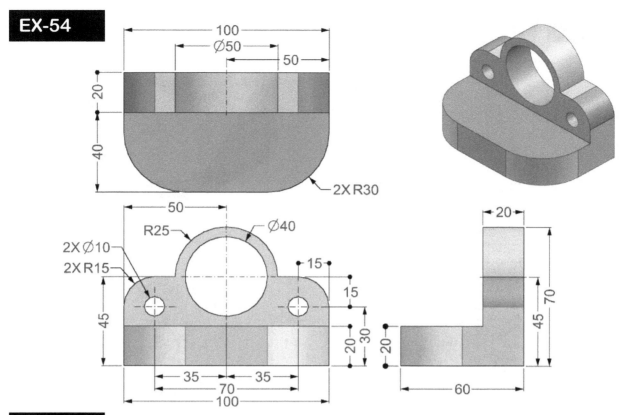

100
Ø50
50
20
40
2X R30

50
R25
Ø40
2X Ø10
2X R15
45
15
15
20
30
35
35
70
100
20
70
45
20
60

EX-55

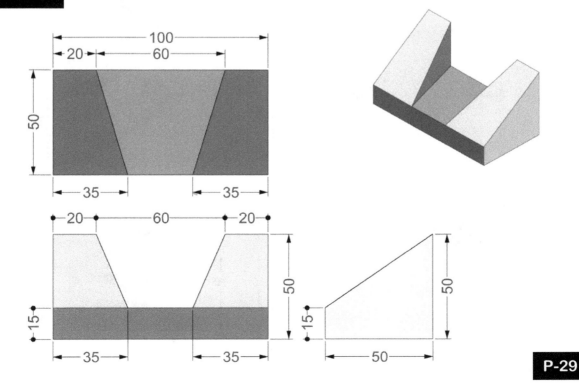

100
20
60
50
35
35

20
60
20
50
15
35
35

50
50
15
50

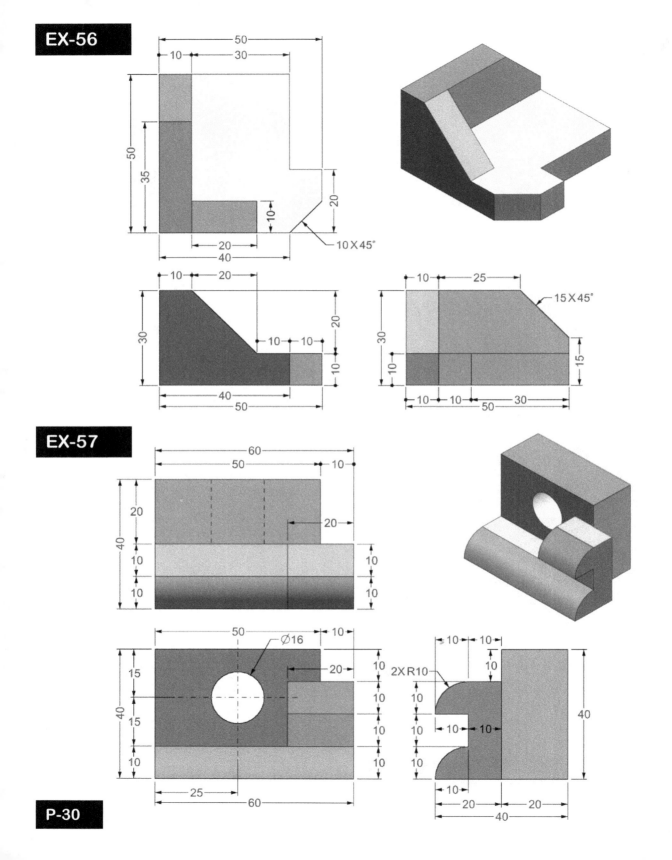

EX-56

EX-57

P-30

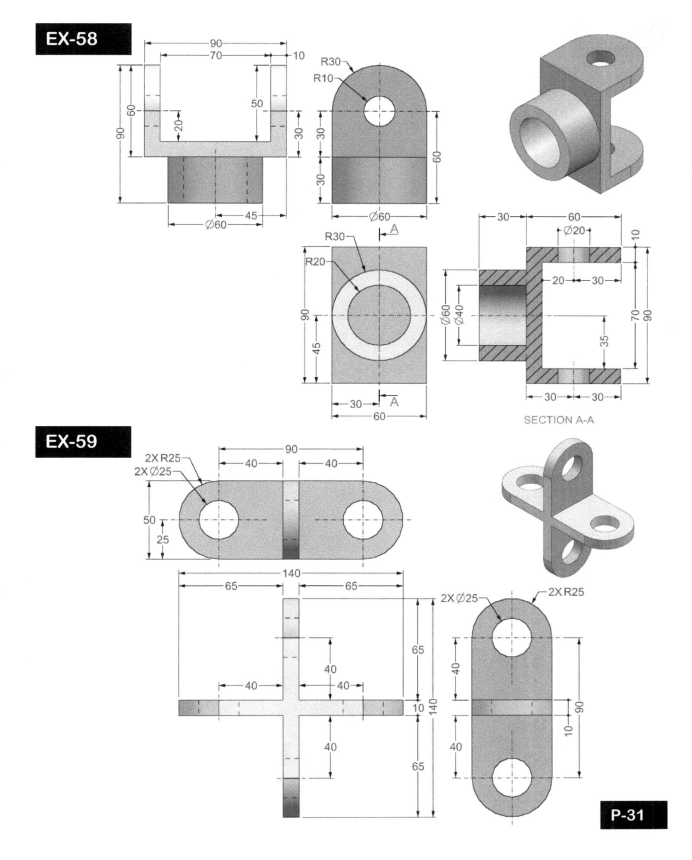

EX-58

90
70
10
60
50
20
90
30
45
Ø60

R30
R10
30
30
60
Ø60
A

R30
R20
90
45
30
60
A

30
60
Ø20
10
20
30
Ø60
Ø40
70
90
35
30
30
SECTION A-A

EX-59

2X R25
2X Ø25
90
40
40
50
25

140
65
65
65
40
40
40
10
40
65

2X Ø25
2X R25
40
90
10
40

P-31

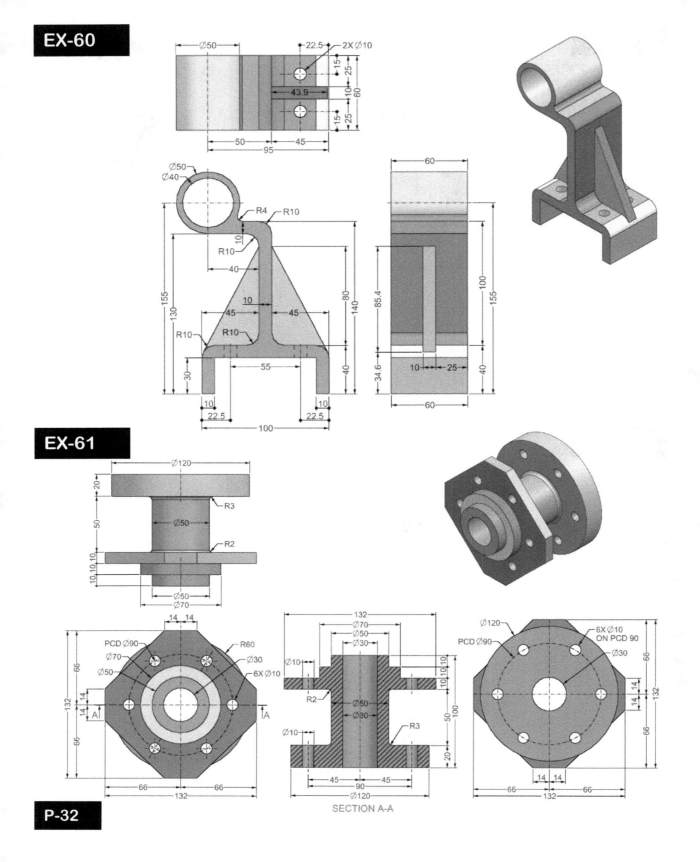

EX-60

EX-61

P-32

SECTION A-A

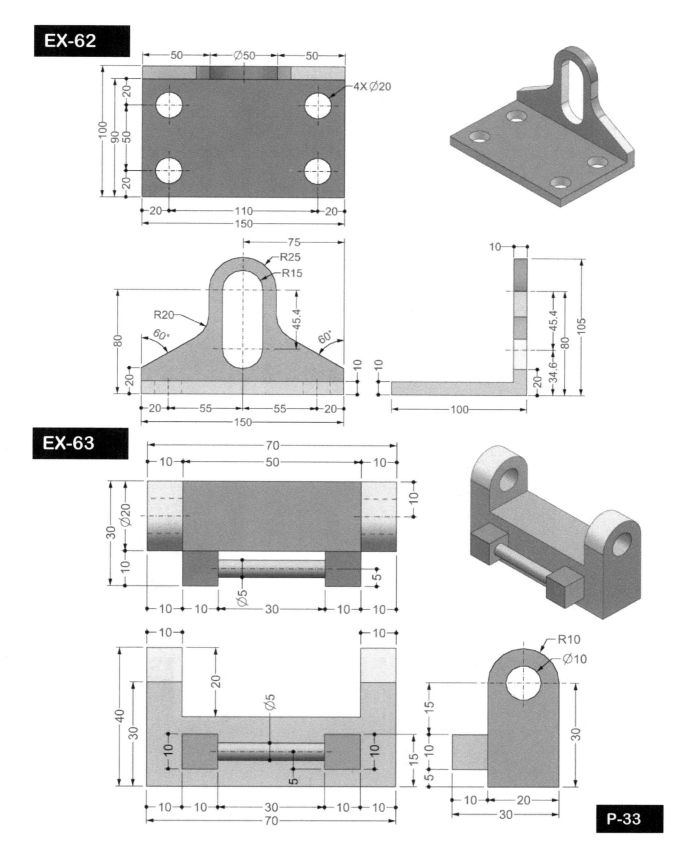

EX-62

EX-63

P-33

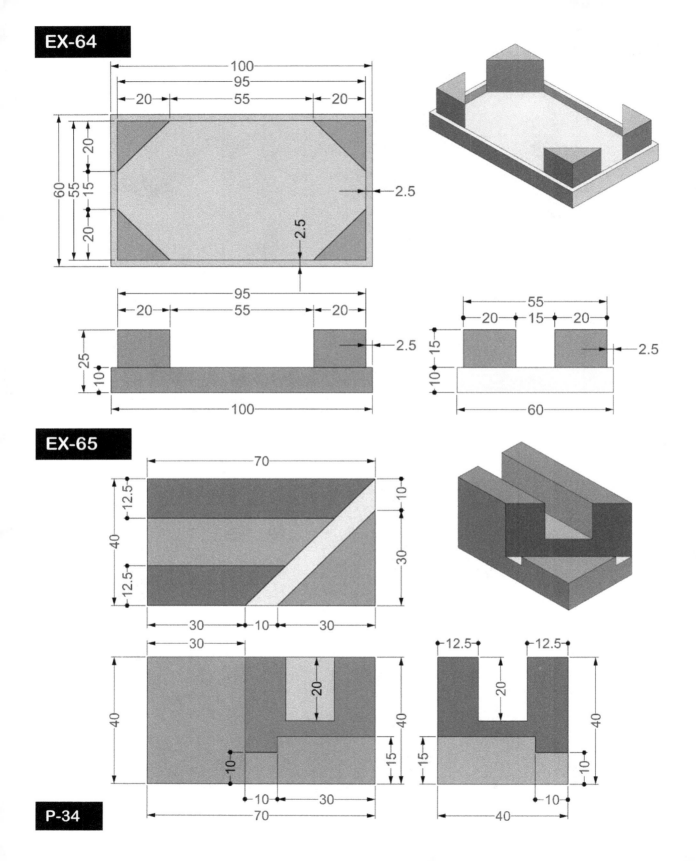

EX-64

EX-65

P-34

EX-66

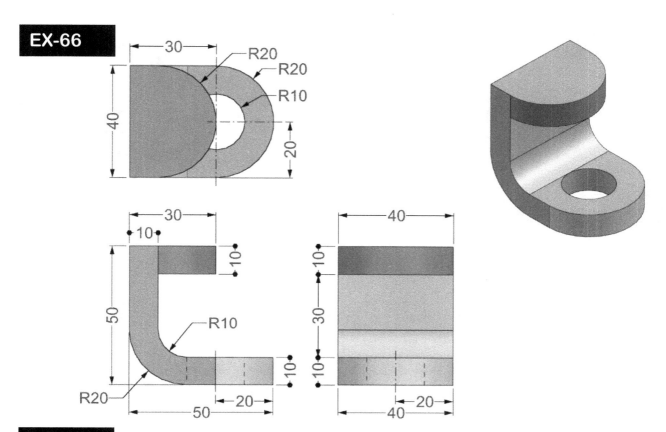

EX-67

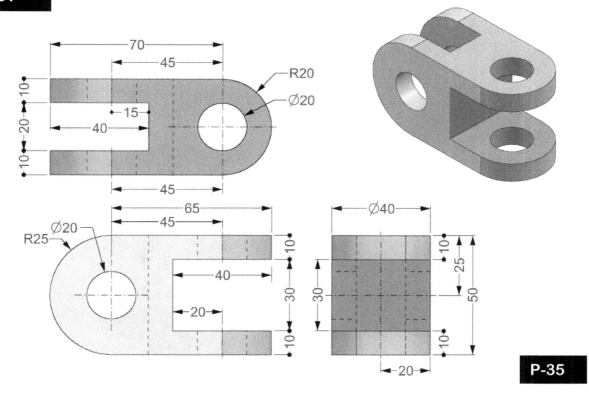

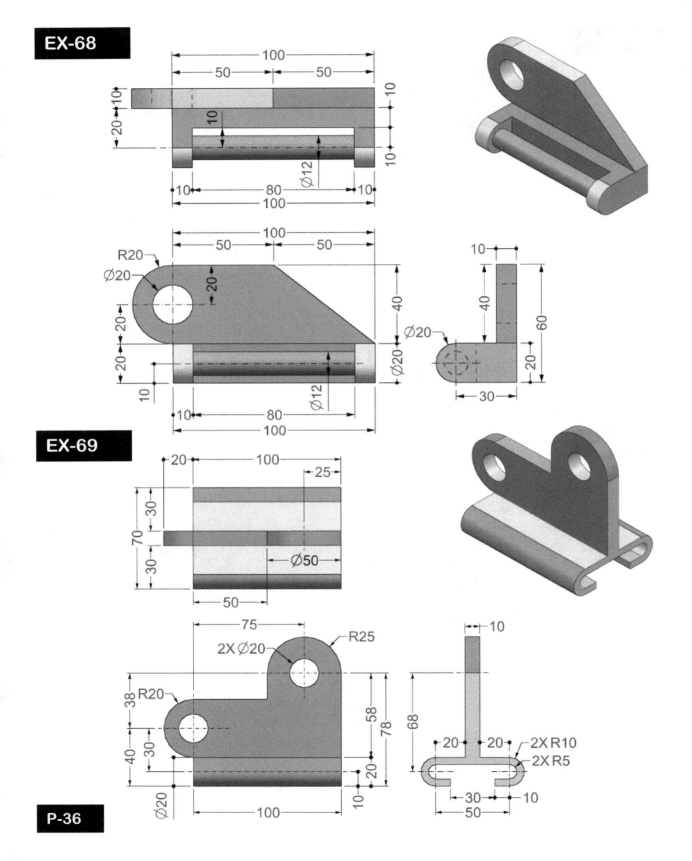

EX-68

EX-69

P-36

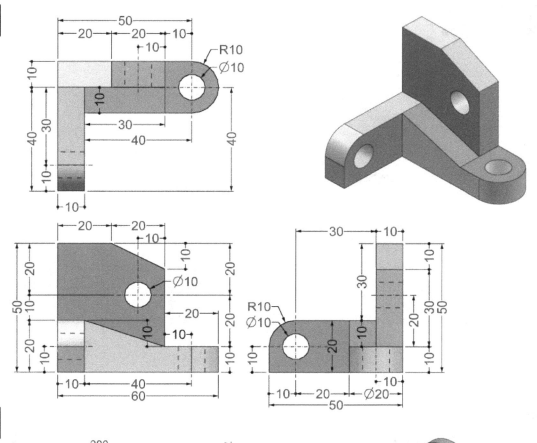

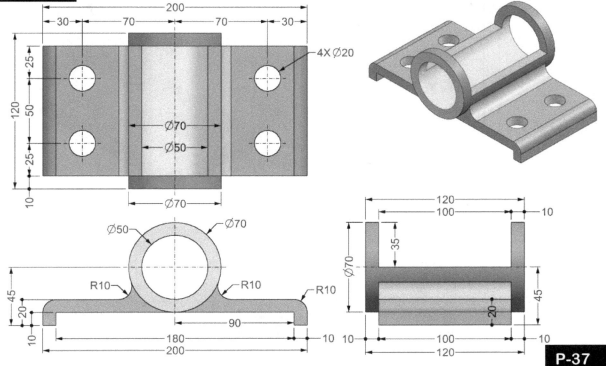

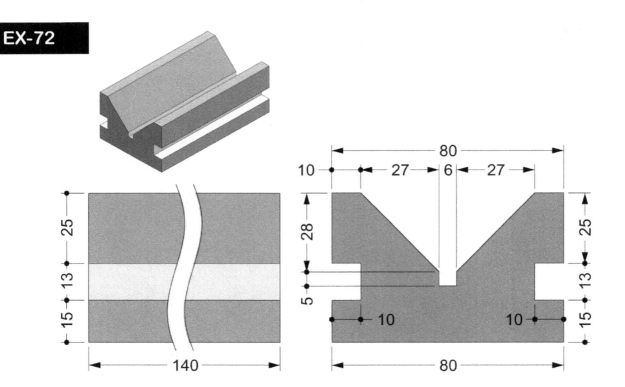

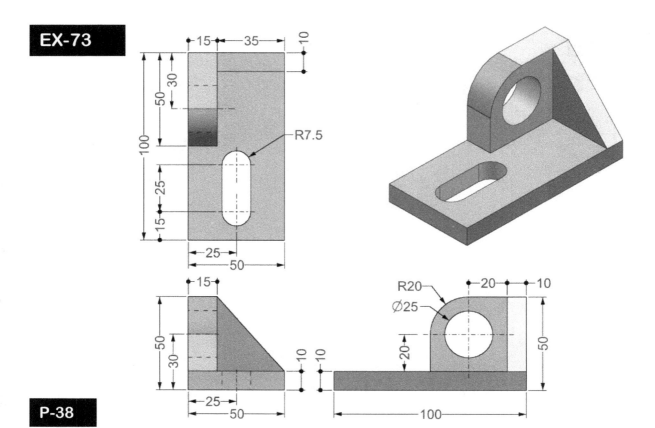

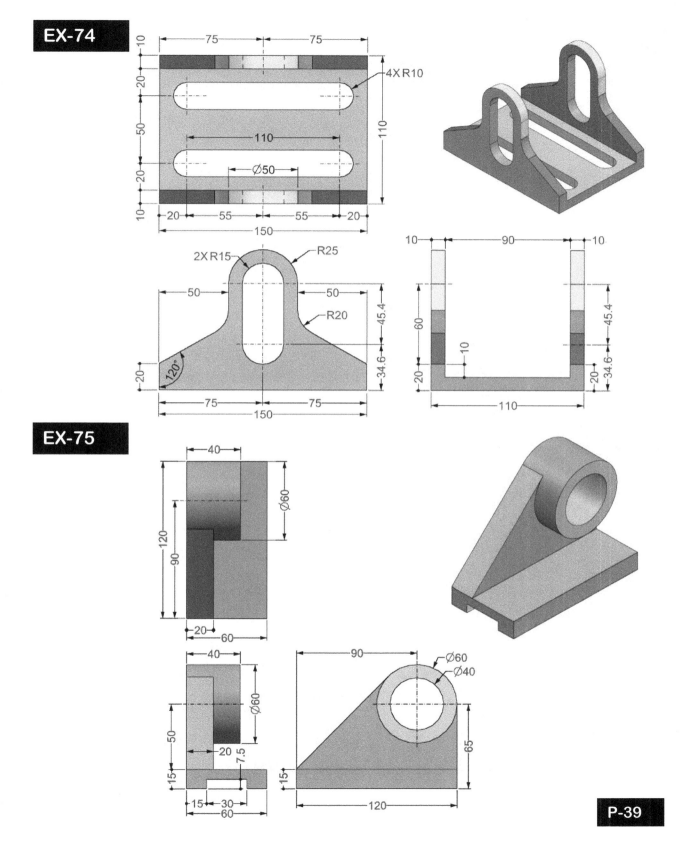

EX-74

4X R10

110

Ø50

2X R15   R25

R20

45.4

34.6

120°

150

60

10

45.4

34.6

110

EX-75

40

Ø60

120

90

20

60

40

Ø60

50

20

7.5

15

15 30

60

90

Ø60
Ø40

65

15

120

P-39

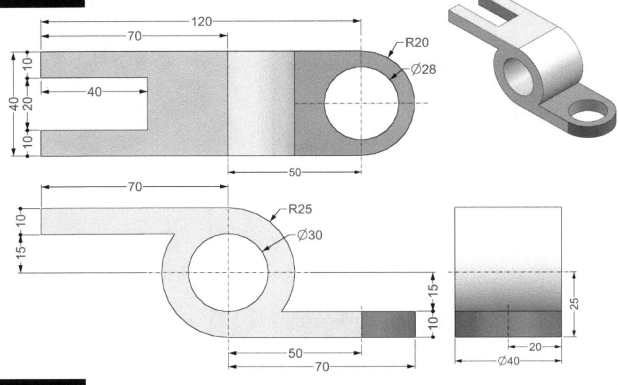

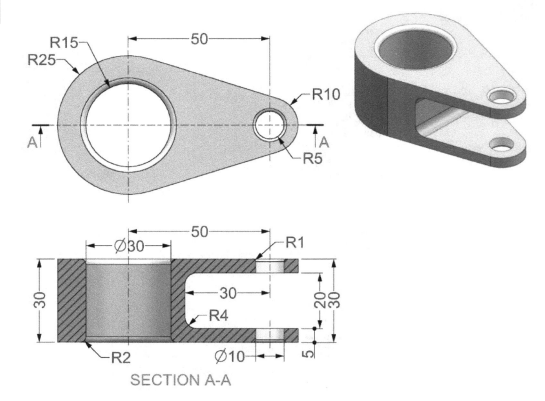

SECTION A-A

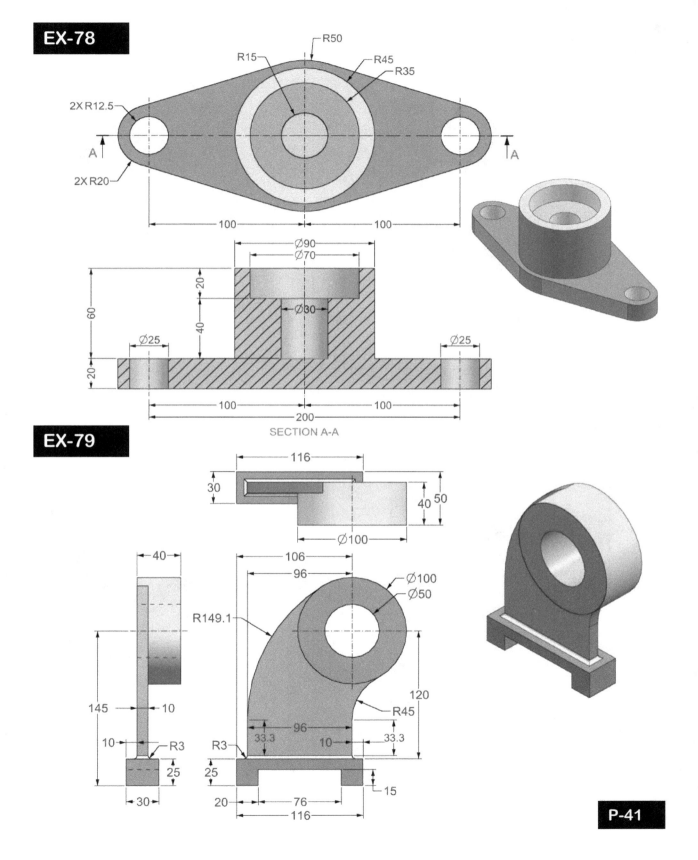

EX-78

R50
R15
R45
R35
2X R12.5
2X R20
A
A
100
100

Ø90
Ø70
20
60
40
Ø30
Ø25
Ø25
20
100
100
200
SECTION A-A

EX-79

116
30
40 50
Ø100

40
106
96
Ø100
Ø50
R149.1
120
R45
145   10
96
10   R3
33.3   96   10   33.3
R3
25
25
15
30
20   76
116

P-41

EX-80

6 HOLES, Ø10
ON DIA 32 PCD

4 HOLES, Ø8.6
ON DIA 54 PCD

Ø70

Ø16

A

A

Ø54

Ø32

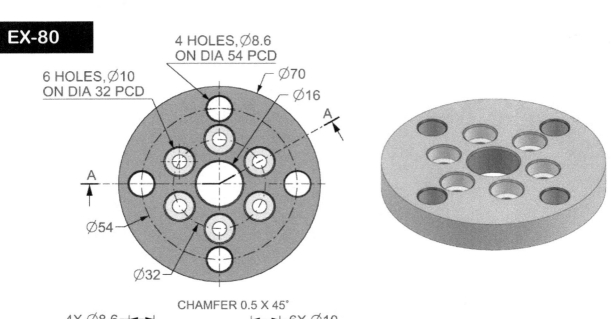

CHAMFER 0.5 X 45°

4X Ø8.6

Ø16

6X Ø10

10

5

5

SECTION A-A
(SCALE 1:1)

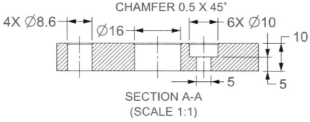

EX-81

10

6X Ø8.4

207.2

171.6

17.8

87.2

4X R19.4

19.2

9.6

106

254

233.6

190.4

254

109.8

56.4

36.6

38 28

10

2X R11.6

60

10

103.6

147.2

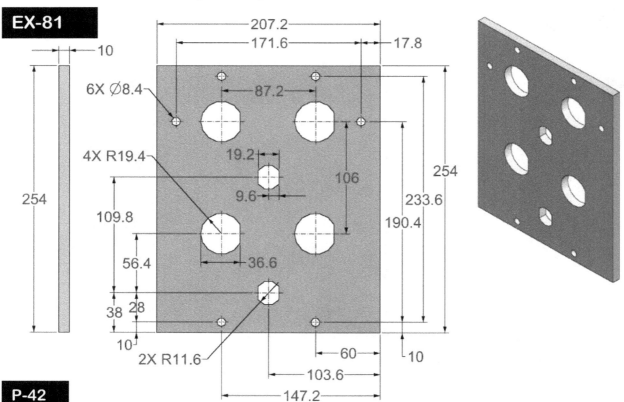

P-42

EX-82

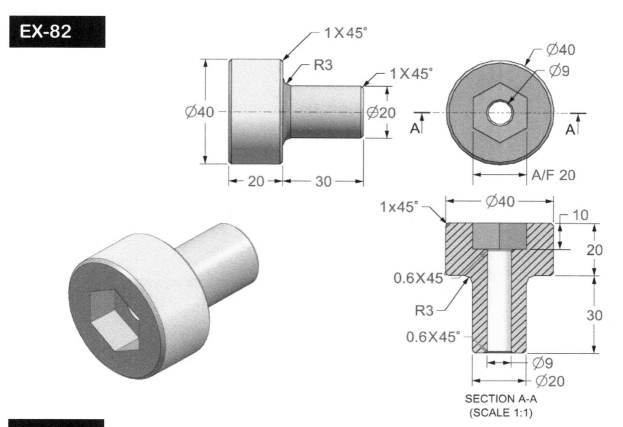

1 X 45°
R3
1 X 45°
Ø40
Ø20
Ø40
Ø9
A/F 20
20
30

1x45°
Ø40
10
20
0.6X45°
R3
30
0.6X45°
Ø9
Ø20

SECTION A-A
(SCALE 1:1)

EX-83

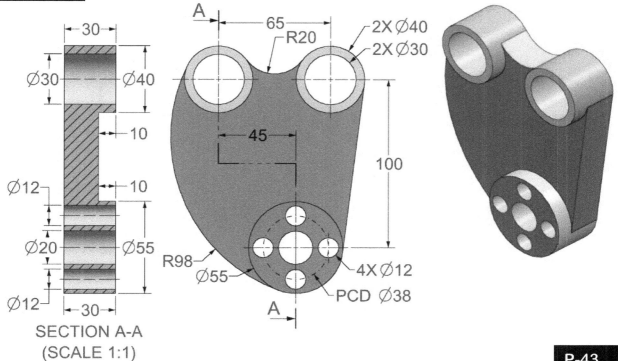

30
Ø30
Ø40
10
10
Ø12
Ø20
Ø55
Ø12
30

SECTION A-A
(SCALE 1:1)

A
65
R20
2X Ø40
2X Ø30
45
100
R98
Ø55
4X Ø12
PCD Ø38
A

EX-84

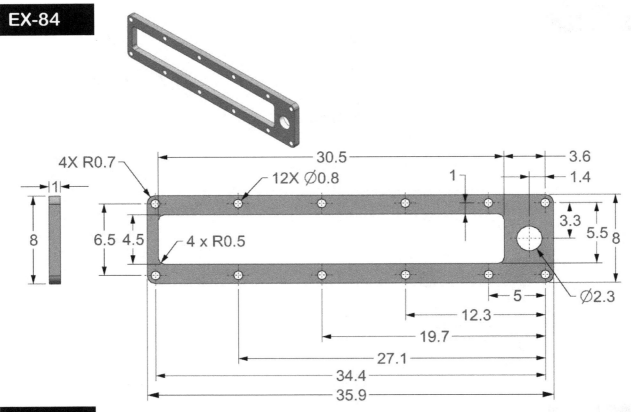

EX-85

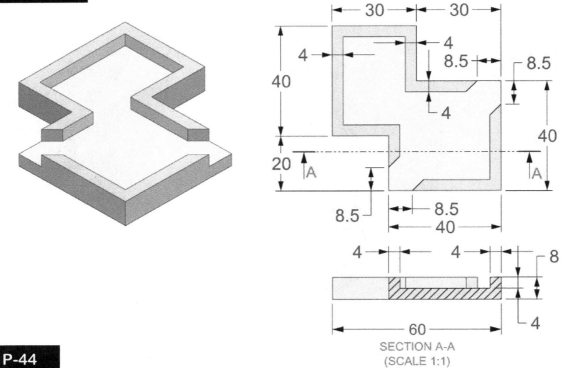

SECTION A-A
(SCALE 1:1)

P-44

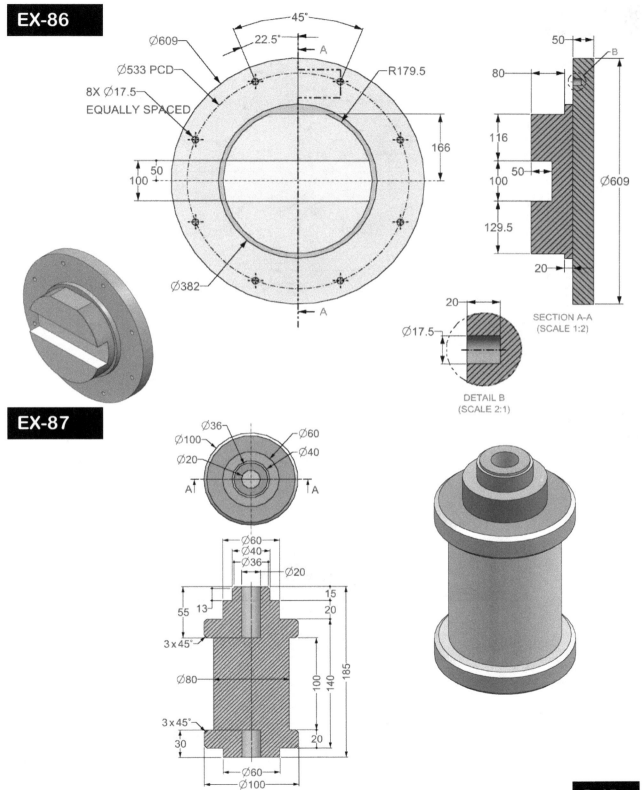

EX-86

Ø609
Ø533 PCD
8X Ø17.5
EQUALLY SPACED
45°
22.5°
A
R179.5
166
50
100
Ø382
A

SECTION A-A
(SCALE 1:2)
50
80
B
116
100
50
129.5
20
Ø609

DETAIL B
(SCALE 2:1)
20
Ø17.5

EX-87

Ø36
Ø100
Ø20
Ø60
Ø40
A   A

SECTION A-A
Ø60
Ø40
Ø36
Ø20
15
55
13
20
3 x 45°
Ø80
100
140
185
Ø20
3 x 45°
30
20
Ø60
Ø100

P-45

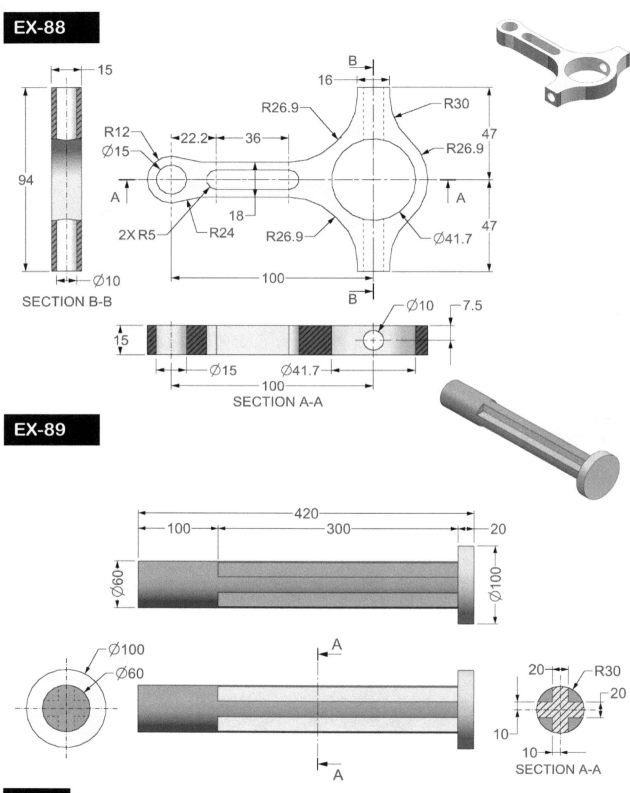

EX-88

15

94

∅10

SECTION B-B

R12
∅15

22.2

36

R26.9

B

16

R30

47

R26.9

47

A

A

2X R5

R24

18

R26.9

∅41.7

100

B

∅10

7.5

15

∅15

∅41.7

100

SECTION A-A

EX-89

420

100

300

20

∅60

∅100

∅100

∅60

A

A

20

R30

20

10

10

SECTION A-A

P-46

EX-90

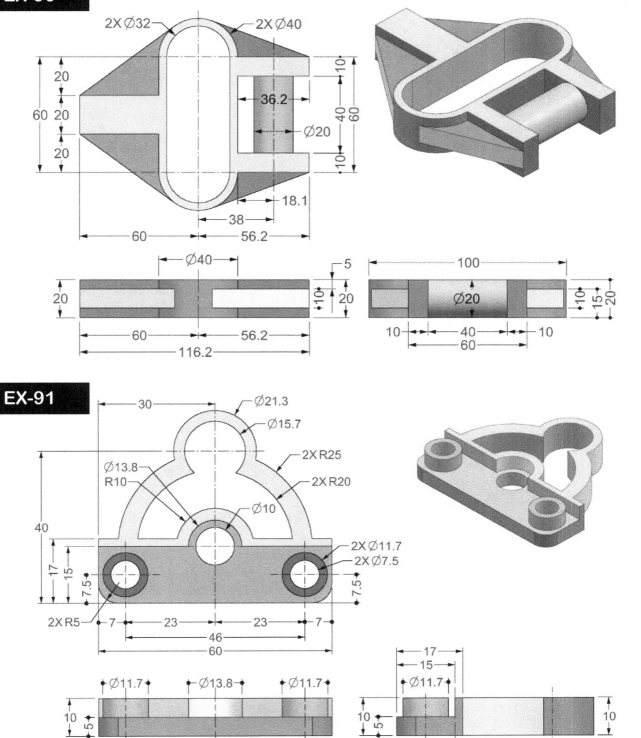

2X Ø32
2X Ø40
20
20
20
60
36.2
Ø20
10
40
60
10
18.1
38
60
56.2
Ø40
20
10
20
5
60
56.2
116.2
100
Ø20
10
15
20
10
40
10
60

EX-91

30
Ø21.3
Ø15.7
2X R25
Ø13.8
R10
2X R20
Ø10
40
17
15
7.5
2X Ø11.7
2X Ø7.5
7.5
2X R5
7
23
23
7
46
60

Ø11.7
Ø13.8
Ø11.7
10
5
7
23
23
7
60

17
15
Ø11.7
10
5
7.5
25
40
10

P-47

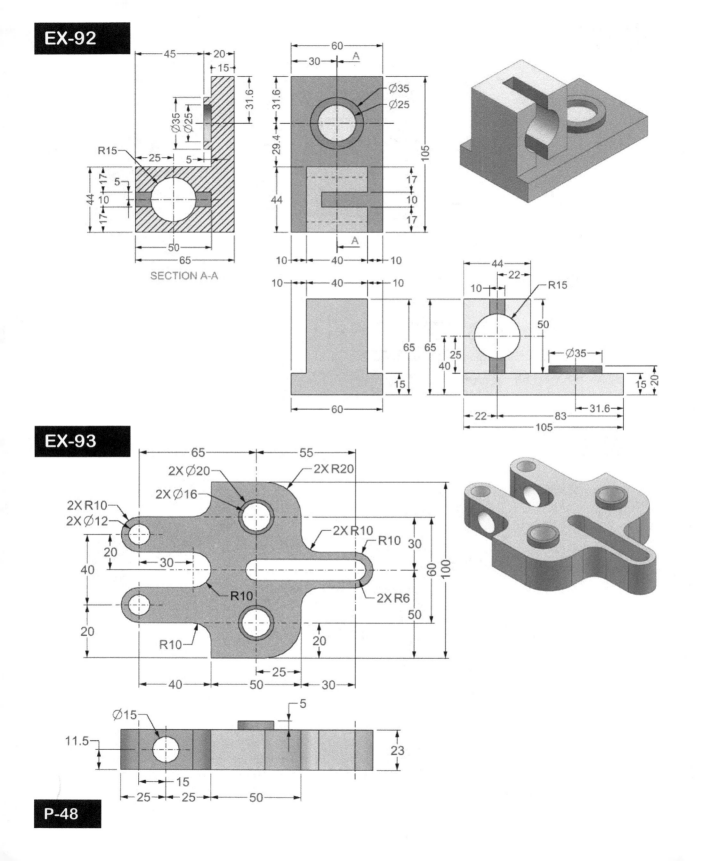

EX-92

SECTION A-A

EX-93

P-48

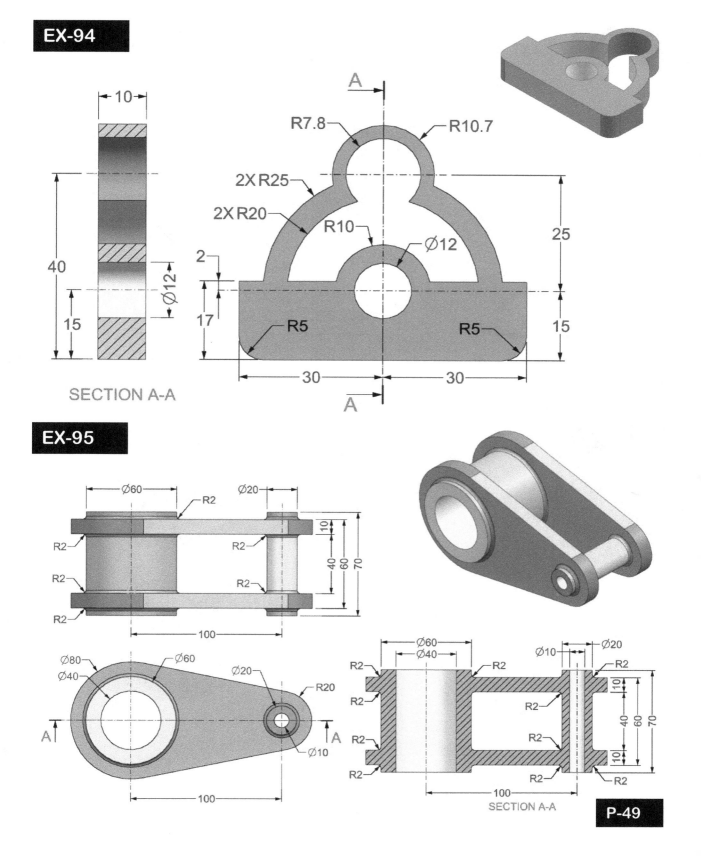

EX-94

10

40

15

∅12

SECTION A-A

A

R7.8   R10.7

2X R25

2X R20

R10   ∅12

25

2

17

R5   R5

15

30   30

A

EX-95

∅60   ∅20   R2

R2

R2   R2

10

40   60   70

R2

R2

100

∅80   ∅60   ∅20   R20

∅40   R2

A   A

∅10

100

∅60   ∅20

∅40   R2   ∅10   R2

R2   R2

R2   10

40   60   70

R2   R2

R2   10

R2   R2   R2

100

SECTION A-A

P-49

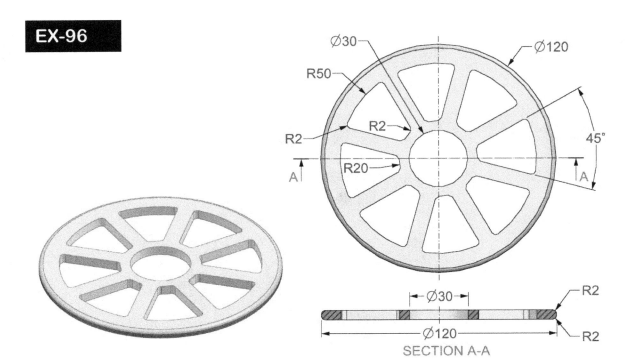

Ø30
Ø120
R50
R2
R2
R20
45°
A
A

Ø30
Ø120
R2
R2
SECTION A-A

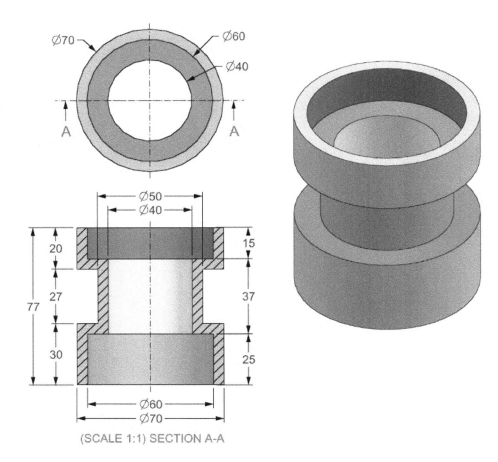

Ø70
Ø60
Ø40
A
A

Ø50
Ø40
20
15
27
37
77
30
25
Ø60
Ø70
(SCALE 1:1) SECTION A-A

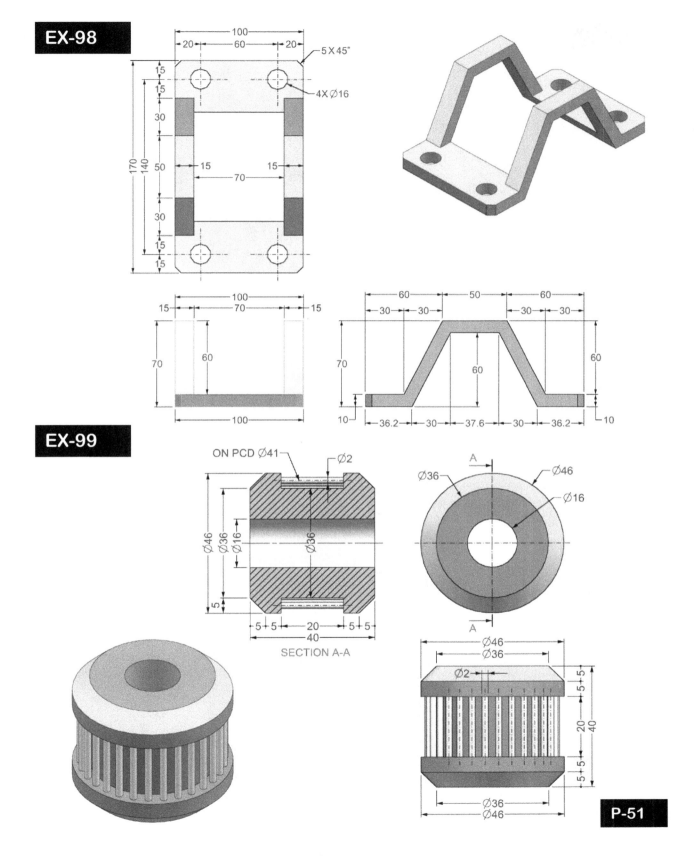

EX-98

100
20 · 60 · 20
5 X 45°
15
15
30
4X Ø16
170
140
50
15 · 15
70
30
15
15

100
15 · 70 · 15
70
60
100

60 · 50 · 60
30 · 30 · 30 · 30
70
60
60
10
36.2 · 30 · 37.6 · 30 · 36.2
10

EX-99

ON PCD Ø41
Ø2
Ø46
A
Ø36
Ø46
Ø16
Ø36
Ø36
Ø16
Ø36
5
5 · 5 · 20 · 5 · 5
40
SECTION A-A
A

Ø46
Ø36
Ø2
5 · 5
20
40
5 · 5
Ø36
Ø46

P-51

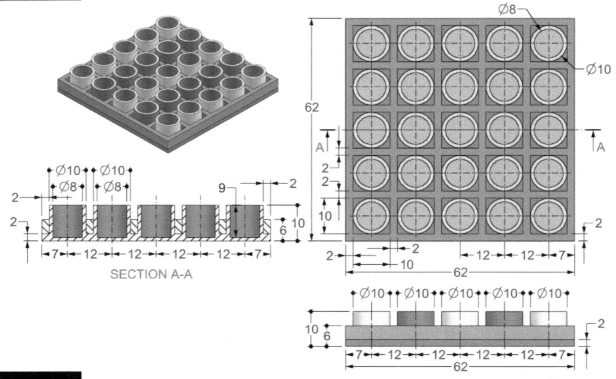

SECTION A-A

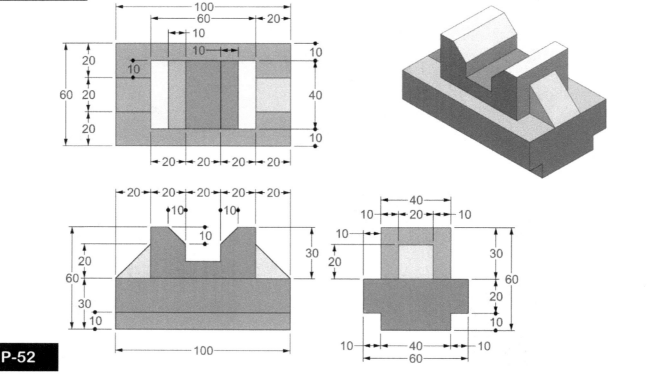

EX-102

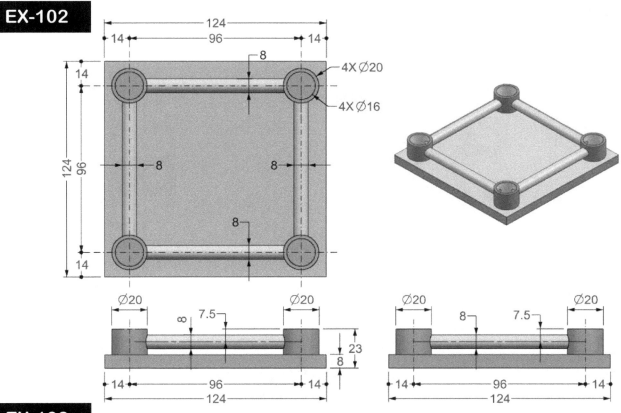

EX-103

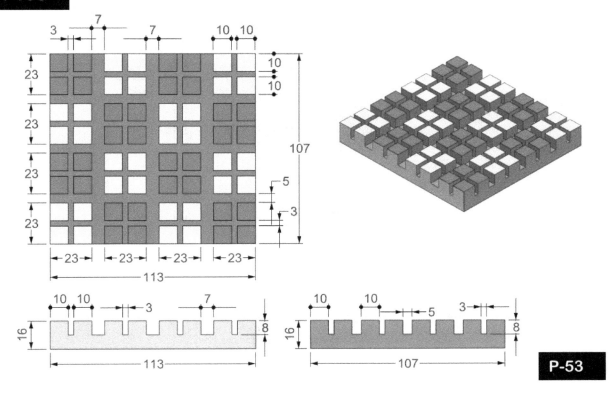

EX-104

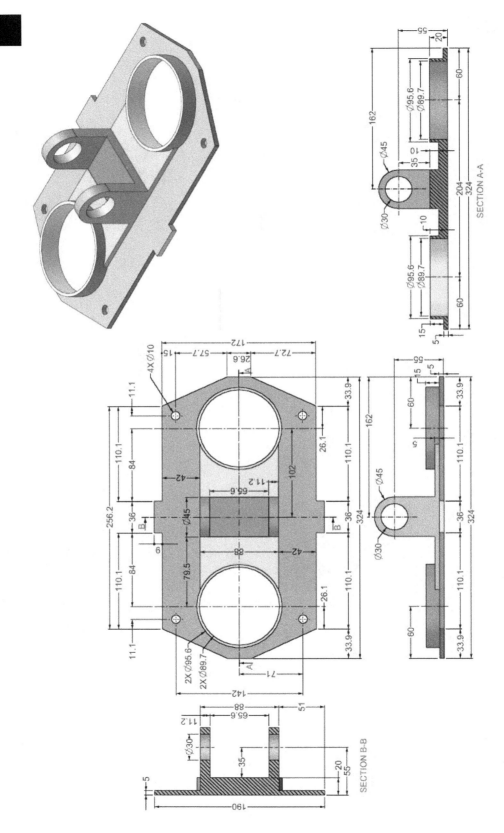

P-54

EX-105

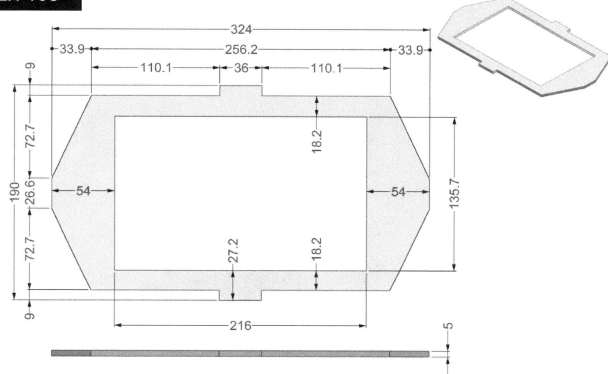

EX-106

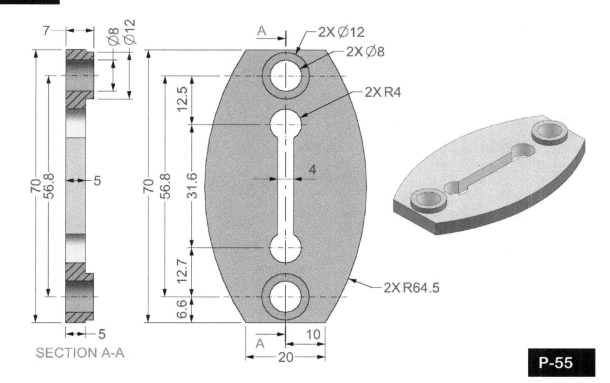

SECTION A-A

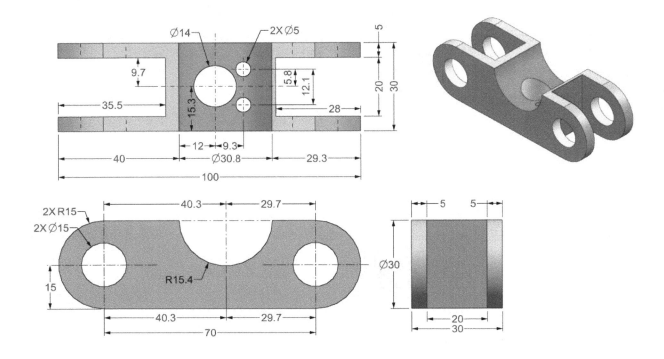

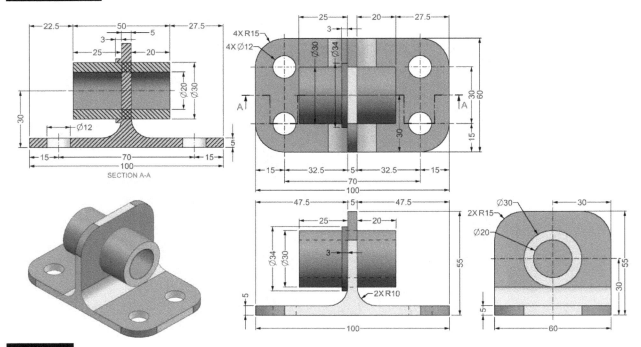

SECTION A-A

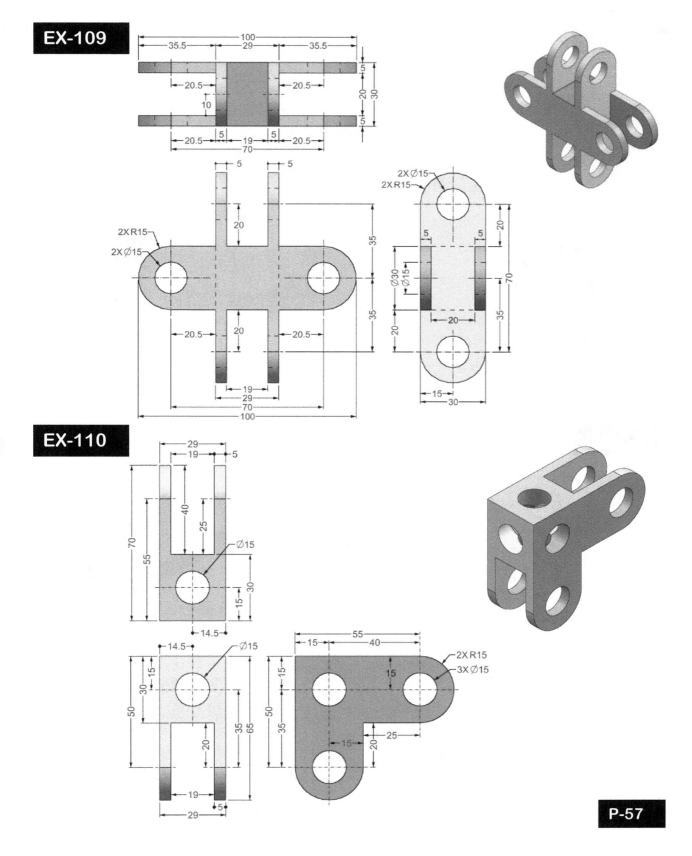

EX-109

EX-110

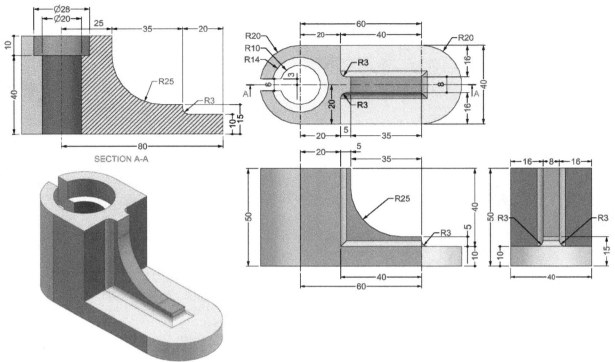

SECTION A-A

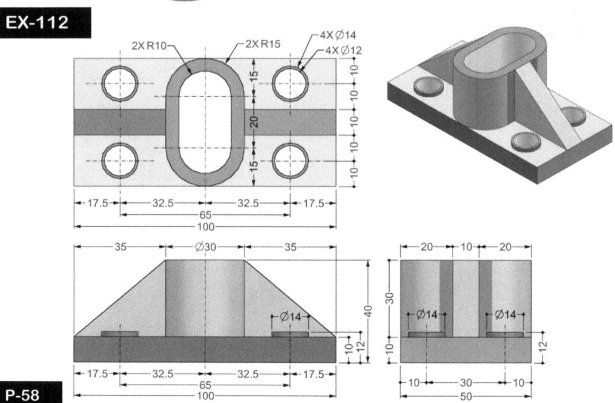

EX-113

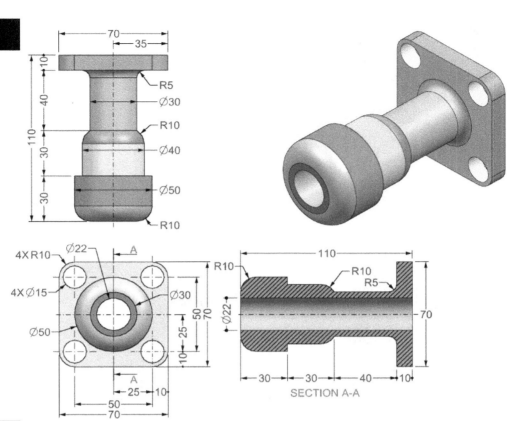

- 70
- 35
- 10
- 40
- 110
- 30
- 30
- R5
- Ø30
- R10
- Ø40
- Ø50
- R10

- 4X R10
- Ø22
- A
- 4X Ø15
- Ø30
- Ø50
- 50
- 70
- 25
- 10
- A
- 25
- 10
- 50
- 70

- 110
- R10
- R10
- R5
- Ø22
- 70
- 30
- 30
- 40
- 10

SECTION A-A

EX-114

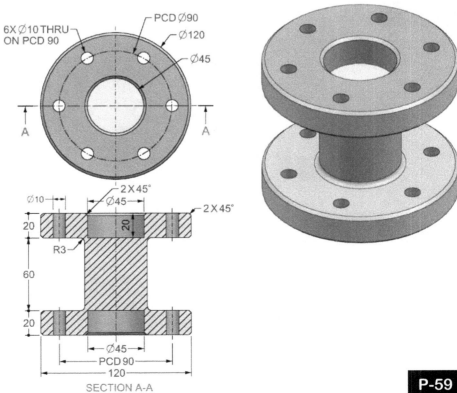

- 6X Ø10 THRU ON PCD 90
- PCD Ø90
- Ø120
- Ø45
- A
- A
- Ø10
- 2 X 45°
- Ø45
- 2 X 45°
- 20
- 20
- R3
- 60
- 20
- Ø45
- PCD 90
- 120

SECTION A-A

EX-115

Ø120
6X Ø10
6X Ø8
PCD Ø90
Ø68
Ø45

A ←→ A

Ø120
Ø68
R2
Ø10
10
10
20
120
60
20
10
PCD 90

Ø120
PCD 90
Ø68
Ø45
Ø10
40
2 X 45°
20
R3
60
20
Ø8
Ø55
Ø50
R3
20
Ø45
Ø8

SECTION A-A

EX-116

120
100
10
25
50
25
10
4X Ø10
4X R5
25
A
A
25
30
50
15
10
Ø30
Ø20

20
80
50
45
20
R5
120

80
70
20
25
Ø10
30
R5
20
10
100
120

SECTION A-A

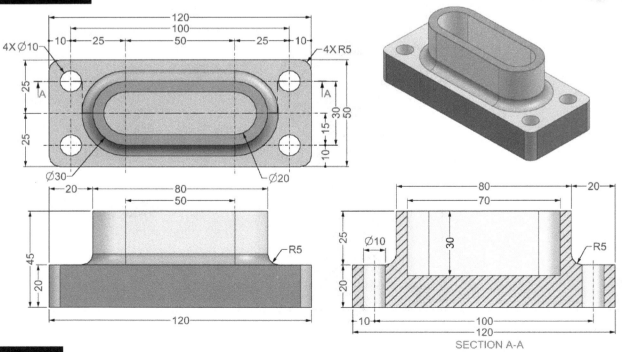

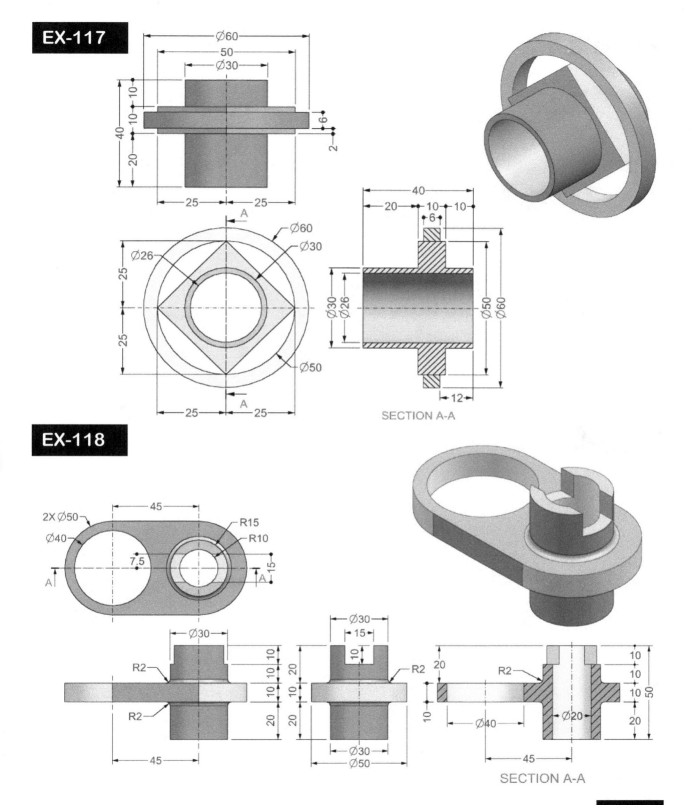

EX-117

Ø60
50
Ø30
40
10
10
20
25 25

A

Ø60
Ø30
Ø26
25
25
25 25
Ø50

A

40
20 10 10
6
Ø30
Ø26
Ø50
Ø60
12

SECTION A-A

EX-118

2X Ø50
Ø40
45
R15
R10
7.5
15
A
A

Ø30
R2
10 10
10 10
10
20
R2
45

Ø30
15
10
20
10
20
R2
Ø30
Ø50

20
R2
10
Ø40
Ø20
45
10
10
10
50
20

SECTION A-A

P-61

EX-119

Ø190
Ø55

2X R20
2X R25
Ø140
70
25
50
Ø55
Ø75
Ø100
Ø180
Ø190

SECTION A-A

A

R25
25
50
A
Ø75
Ø190

Ø75
Ø190
Ø55
Ø180
Ø100

EX-120

Ø50
Ø60
10
15
20
20
20
40
20
20
45
15
100

R15
A
Ø50
Ø70
Ø70
Ø40
Ø20
Ø30
A
Ø60
100
100

Ø50
Ø30
Ø60
Ø40
10
15
20
20
20
Ø20
40
20
15
90
45
100
100
SECTION A-A

P-62

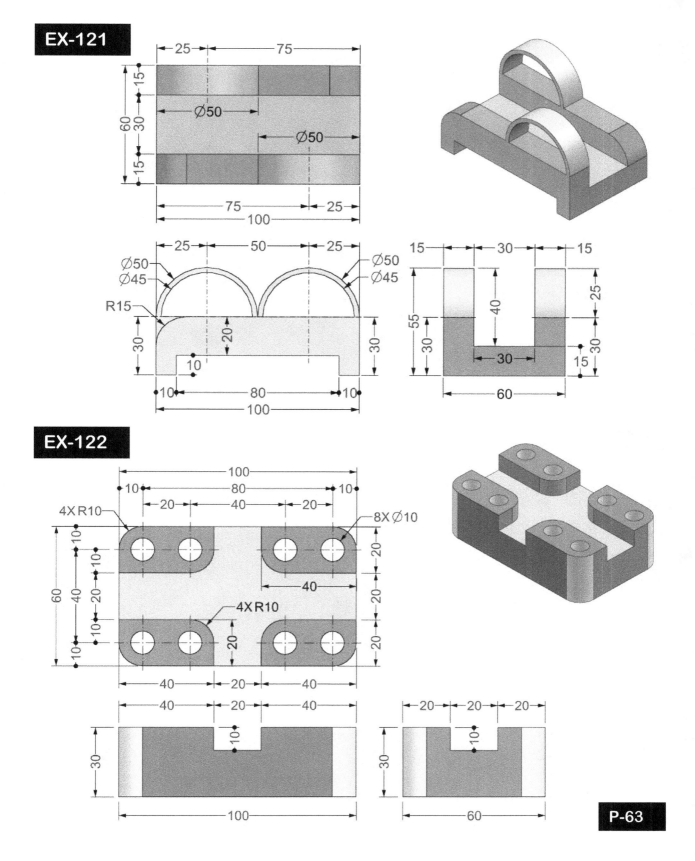

EX-121

EX-122

EX-123

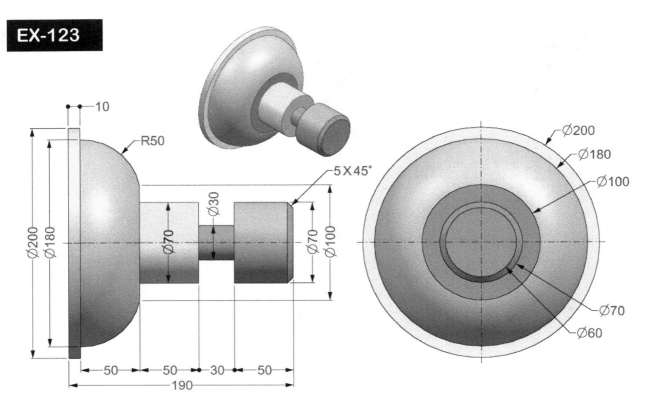

10
R50
5×45°
Ø30
Ø70
Ø70
Ø100
Ø200
Ø180
Ø200
Ø180
Ø100
Ø70
Ø60
50
50
30
50
190

EX-124

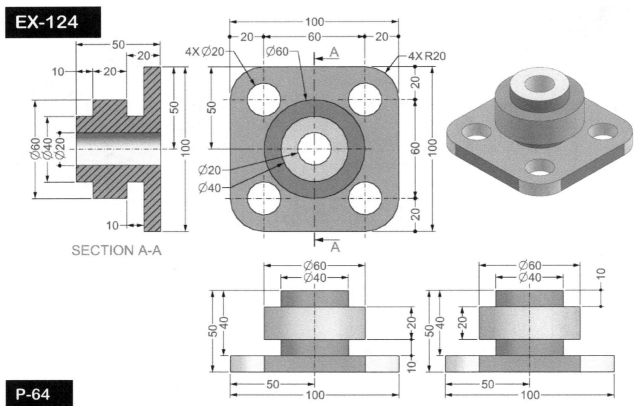

50
20
10
20
Ø60
Ø40
Ø20
50
100
10
SECTION A-A

100
20
60
20
4X Ø20
Ø60
A
4X R20
20
50
60
100
Ø20
Ø40
20
A

Ø60
Ø40
50
40
50
100
Ø60
Ø40
20
10
Ø60
Ø40
10
50
40
20
50
100

P-64

EX-125

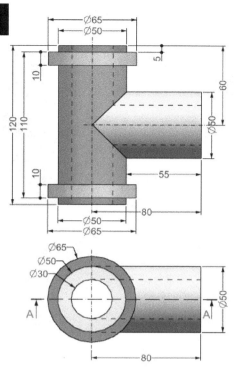

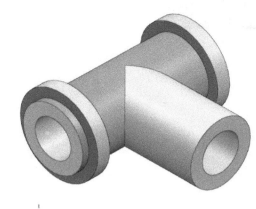

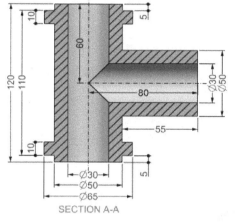

SECTION A-A

EX-126

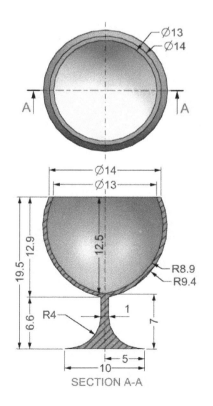

SECTION A-A

P-65

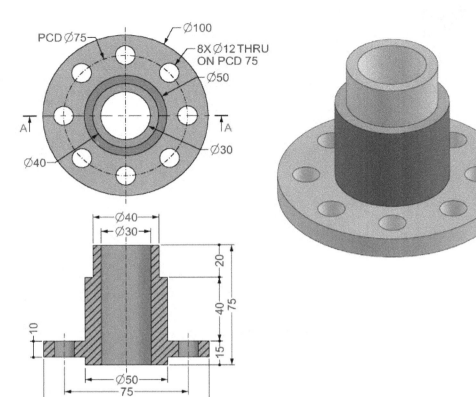

PCD Ø75

Ø100

8X Ø12 THRU
ON PCD 75

Ø50

Ø30

A

A

Ø40

Ø40

Ø30

20

40

75

10

15

Ø50

75

Ø100

SECTION A-A

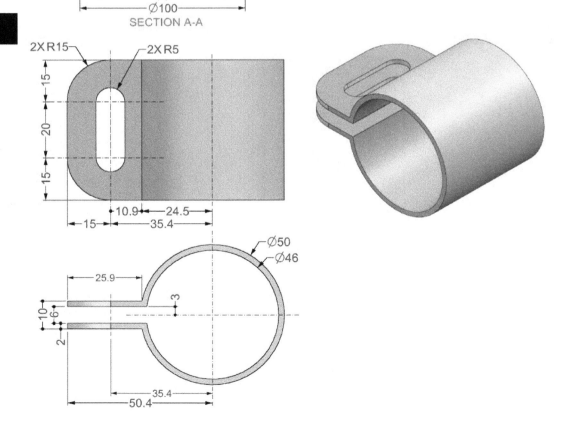

2X R15

2X R5

15

20

15

10.9

24.5

15

35.4

Ø50

Ø46

25.9

3

10

6

2

35.4

50.4

EX-129

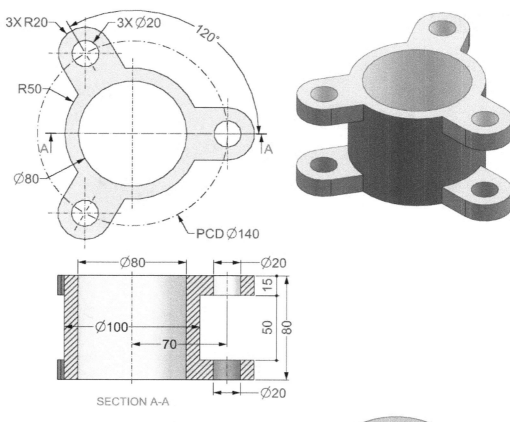

3X R20 3X Ø20 120°
R50
Ø80
PCD Ø140

Ø80 Ø20
Ø100 15
70 50 80
Ø20

SECTION A-A

EX-130

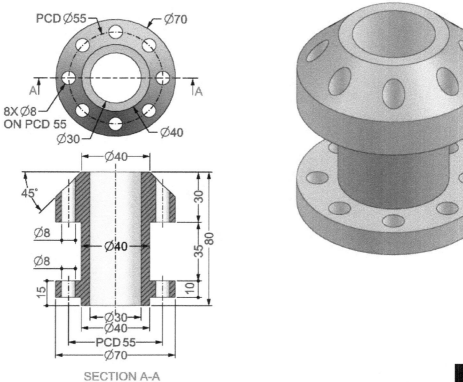

PCD Ø55 Ø70
8X Ø8
ON PCD 55
Ø30 Ø40

Ø40
45°
Ø8 30
Ø40 80
Ø8 35
15 10
Ø30
Ø40
PCD 55
Ø70

SECTION A-A

EX-131

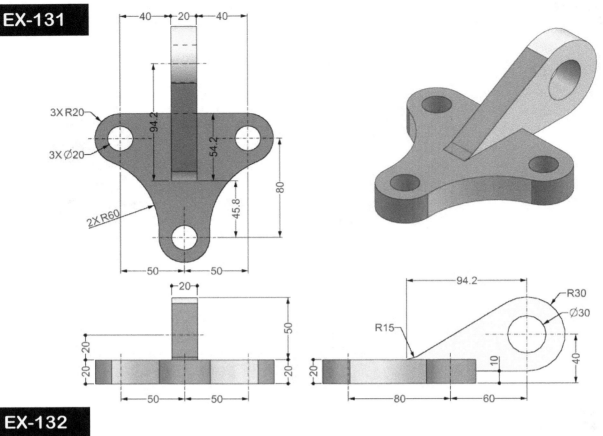

EX-132

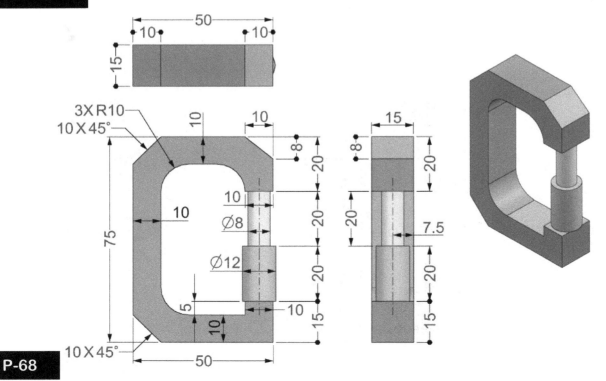

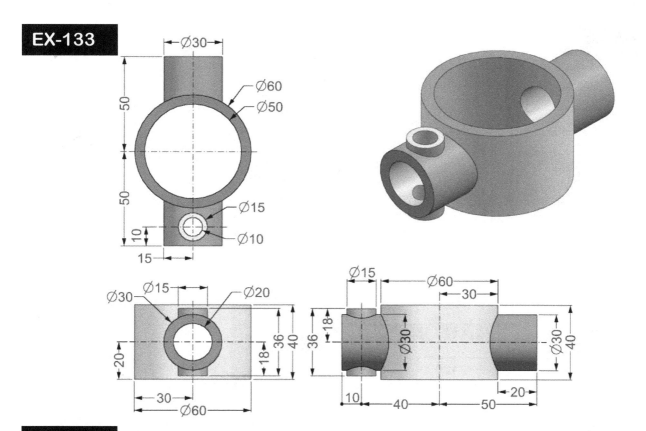

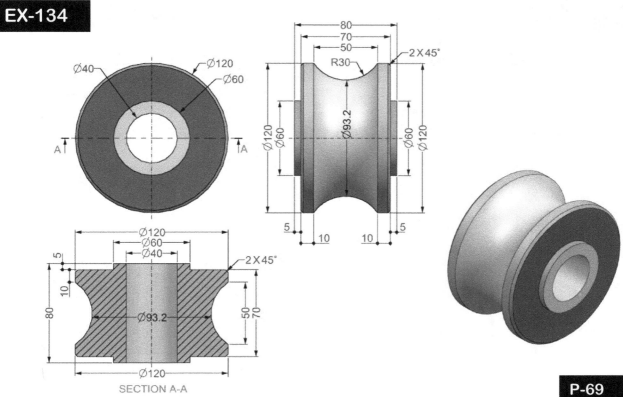

SECTION A-A

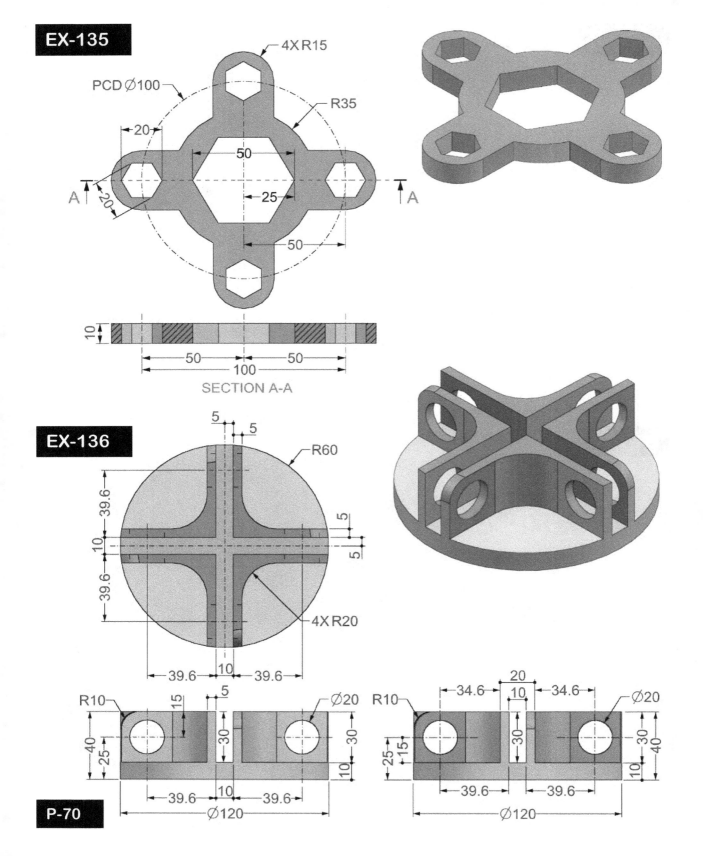

EX-135

4X R15
PCD ∅100
R35
20
50
25
20
50

A — A

SECTION A-A
10
50 — 50
100

EX-136

5
5
R60
39.6
10
5
5
39.6
4X R20
39.6
10
39.6

R10
15
5
∅20
40
25
30
30
39.6
10
39.6
10
∅120

20
10
R10
34.6
34.6
∅20
30
25
15
30
40
10
39.6
39.6
∅120

P-70

EX-137

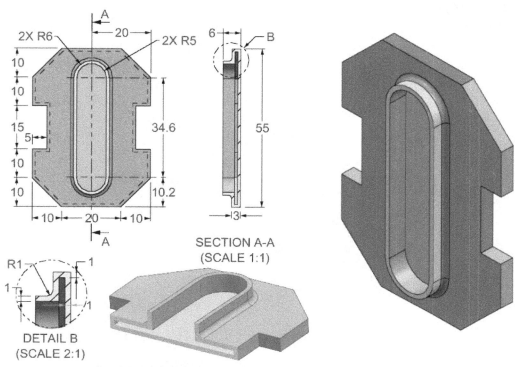

2X R6
2X R5
20
6
B

10
10
15
5
10
10

34.6
10.2

55
3

A
A

SECTION A-A
(SCALE 1:1)

10
20
10

R1
1
1
1

DETAIL B
(SCALE 2:1)

SHELL THICKNESS = 1MM
ALL INSIDE WALL THICKNESS

EX-138

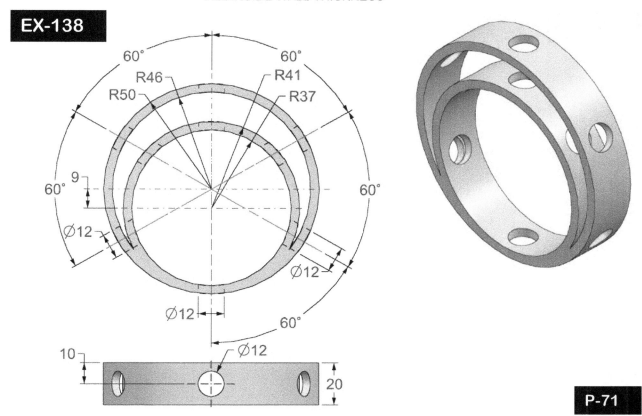

60°
60°
R46
R41
R50
R37

60°
9
60°

Ø12
Ø12
Ø12
60°

10
Ø12
20

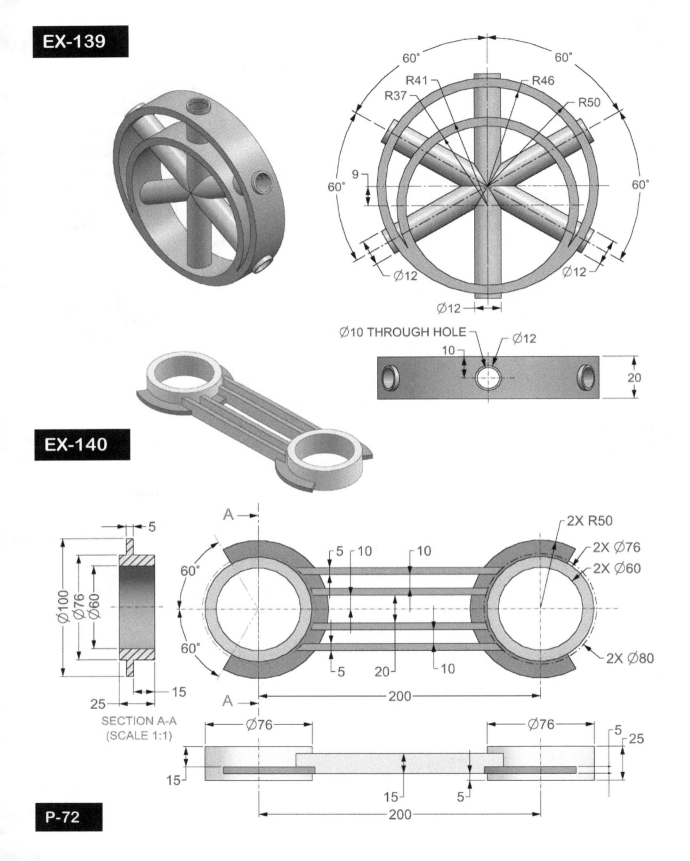

EX-139

R41
R37
R46
R50
60°
60°
60°
60°
9
Ø12
Ø12
Ø12

Ø10 THROUGH HOLE — Ø12
10
20

EX-140

A

5
60°
Ø100
Ø76
Ø60
60°
15
25
SECTION A-A
(SCALE 1:1)
A

5 10   10
2X R50
2X Ø76
2X Ø60

5   20   10
2X Ø80
200

Ø76   Ø76
5 25
15   15   5
200

P-72

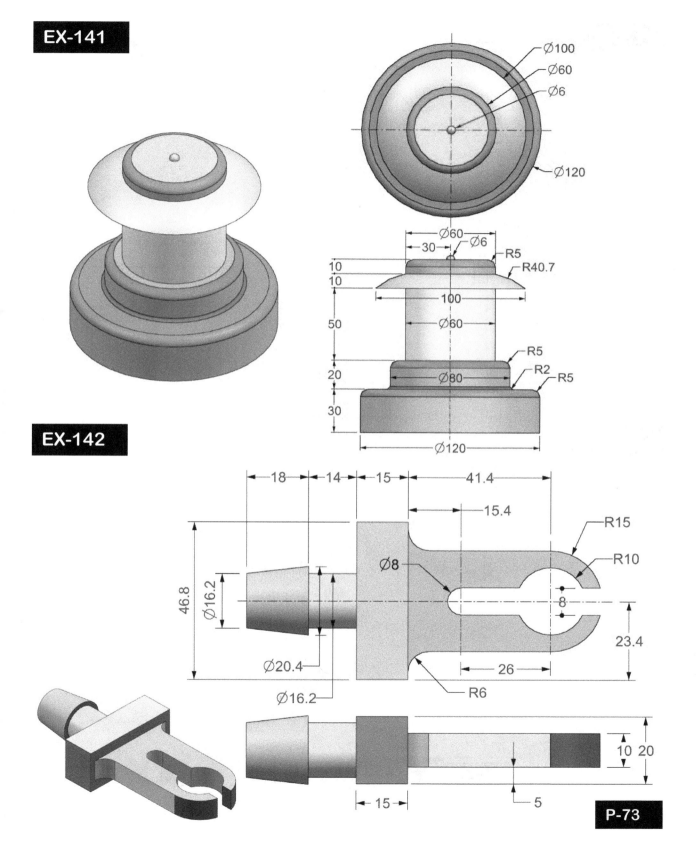

EX-141

Ø100
Ø60
Ø6
Ø120

Ø60
30
Ø6
R5
R40.7
10
10
100
50
Ø60
R5
20
Ø80
R2
R5
30
Ø120

EX-142

18
14
15
41.4
15.4
R15
R10
Ø8
46.8
Ø16.2
8
Ø20.4
23.4
26
Ø16.2
R6

10 20

15
5

P-73

EX-143

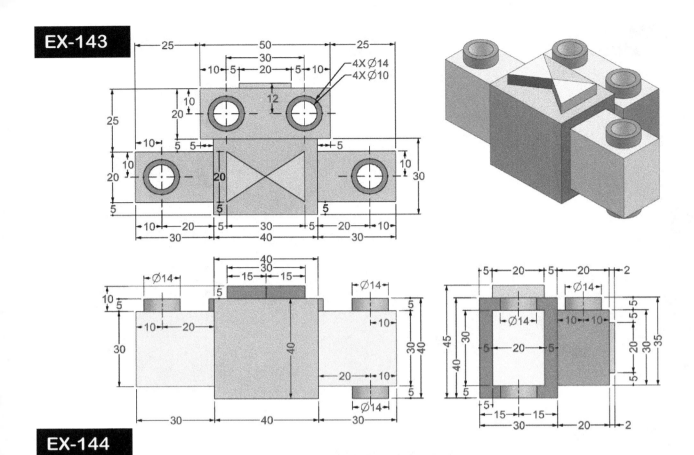

EX-144

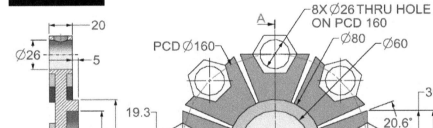

8X Ø26 THRU HOLE
ON PCD 160

PCD Ø160
Ø80 Ø60

SECTION A-A

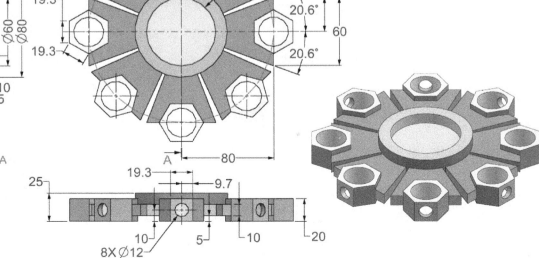

25
19.3
9.7
10
5
10
20
8X Ø12

P-74

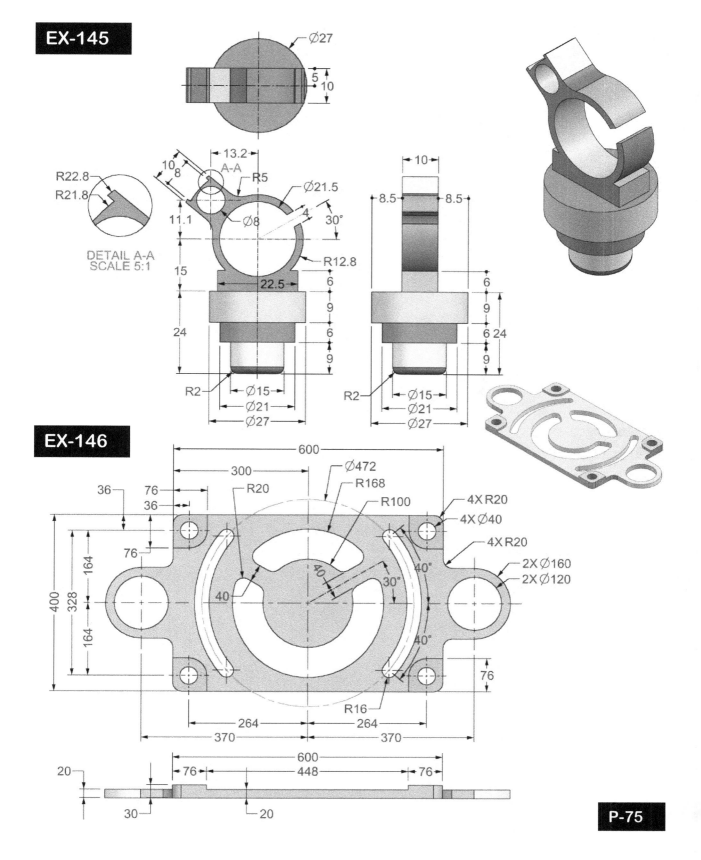

EX-145

⌀27
5
10

R22.8
R21.8

DETAIL A-A
SCALE 5:1

13.2
10
8
A-A
R5
⌀21.5
11.1
⌀8
4
30°
15
22.5
R12.8
24
R2
⌀15
⌀21
⌀27

10
8.5 8.5
6
9
6
9
R2
⌀15
⌀21
⌀27
6 24

EX-146

600
300
⌀472
R168
R100
4X R20
4X ⌀40
4X R20
2X ⌀160
2X ⌀120
36
76
36
R20
76
40
40°
30°
40
40°
164
400
328
164
40°
76
264
264
R16
370
370

600
448
76
76
20
76
30
20

P-75

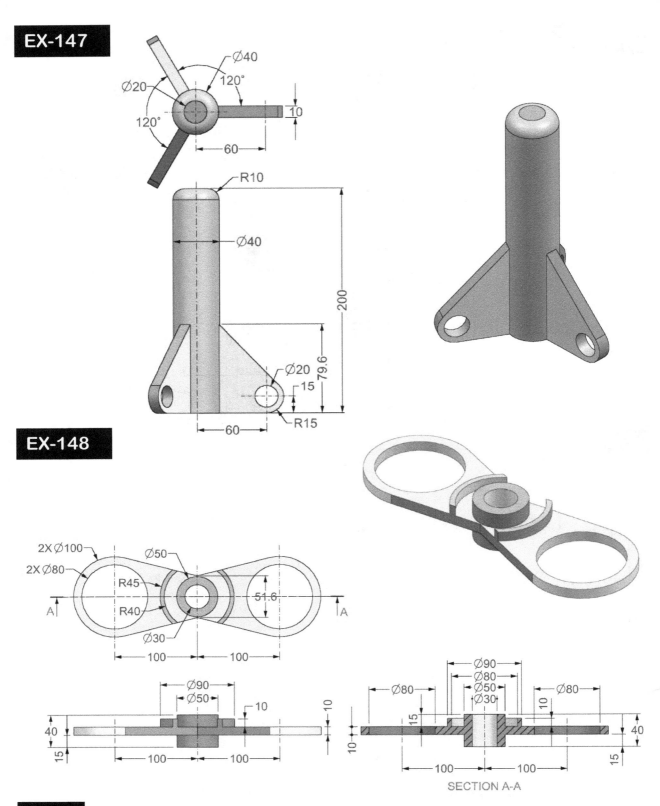

EX-147

Ø40
Ø20
120°
120°
10
60

R10
Ø40
200
79.6
Ø20
15
60
R15

EX-148

2X Ø100
2X Ø80
Ø50
R45
R40
Ø30
51.6
100
100

Ø90
Ø50
10
10
40
15
100
100

Ø90
Ø80
Ø50
Ø30
Ø80
Ø80
10
15
40
10
100
100
15
SECTION A-A

A

A

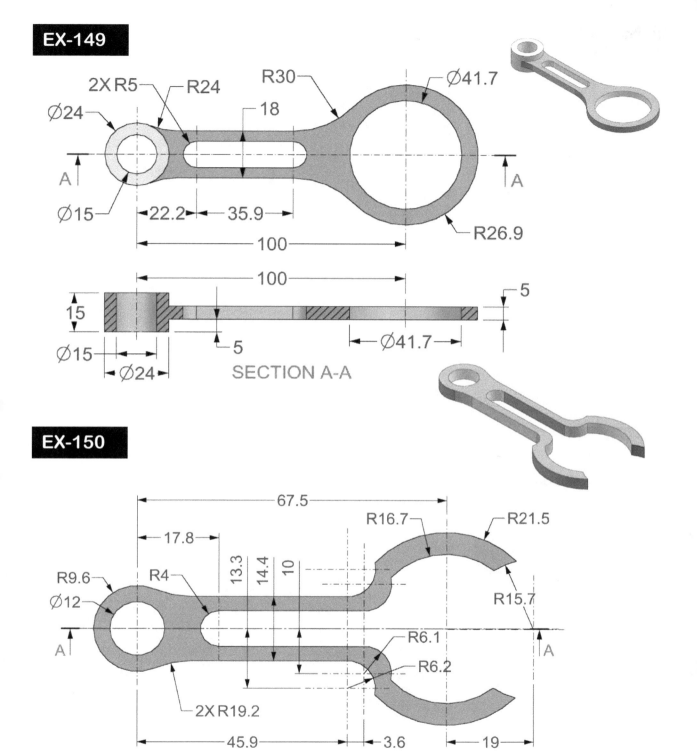

EX-149

2X R5 — R24   R30   Ø41.7
Ø24
18
2X R5
R24
Ø15
22.2   35.9
100

100
15
5
Ø15
Ø24
Ø41.7
R26.9
SECTION A-A

EX-150

67.5
17.8   R16.7   R21.5
R9.6   R4
13.3 14.4 10
Ø12
R15.7
R6.1
R6.2
A
2X R19.2
45.9   3.6   19

5
Ø12   SECTION A-A

EX-151

Ø8
6.5
10
28
R1.5
R1.5
11
B-B
27
Ø10
SECTION A-A

Ø20
A
R3
35
15°
20
5
A
Ø13.3
Ø16

R8
R10
R6.7
R4
R5

1
45°
DETAIL B-B
SCALE 5:1

EX-152

Ø20
Ø36
Ø58
Ø52
Ø16

A

Ø36
Ø20
R8
8
20
2
135°
13.5
Ø16
R11.2
15.8
76
21.6
10.7
13
10
R6
Ø16
R3
SECTION A-A

58
3
R3
R2
Ø52
Ø16
76
R6
A
A
40

P-78

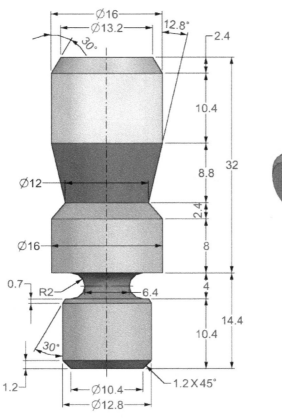

Ø16
Ø13.2
12.8°
30°
2.4
10.4
32
Ø12
8.8
2.4
Ø16
8
0.7
R2
6.4
4
14.4
10.4
30°
1.2
Ø10.4
Ø12.8
1.2 X 45°

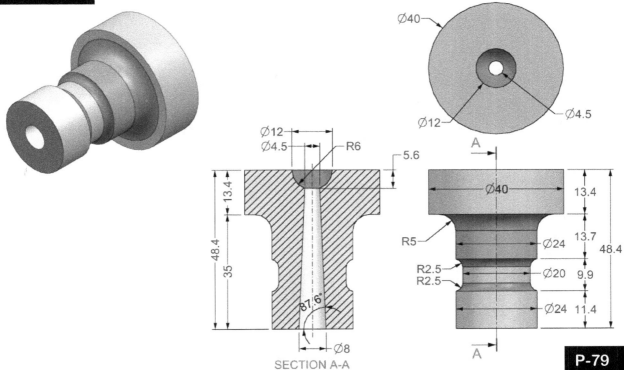

Ø40
Ø12
Ø4.5
A
Ø12
Ø4.5
R6
5.6
13.4
Ø40
13.4
48.4
35
R5
13.7
Ø24
R2.5
Ø20
9.9
R2.5
87.6°
Ø24
11.4
Ø8
48.4
SECTION A-A
A

EX-155

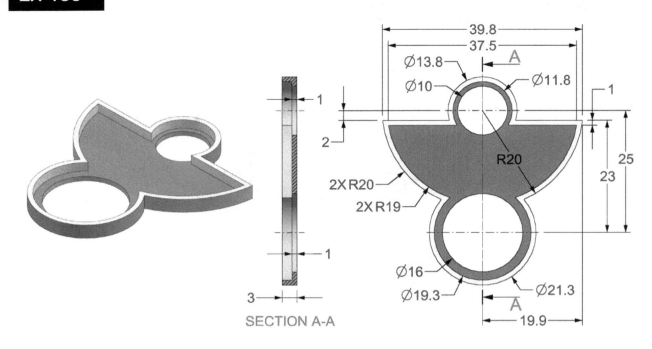

SECTION A-A

EX-156

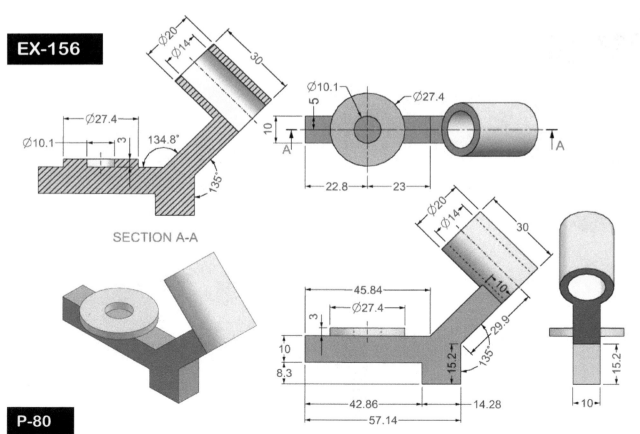

SECTION A-A

P-80

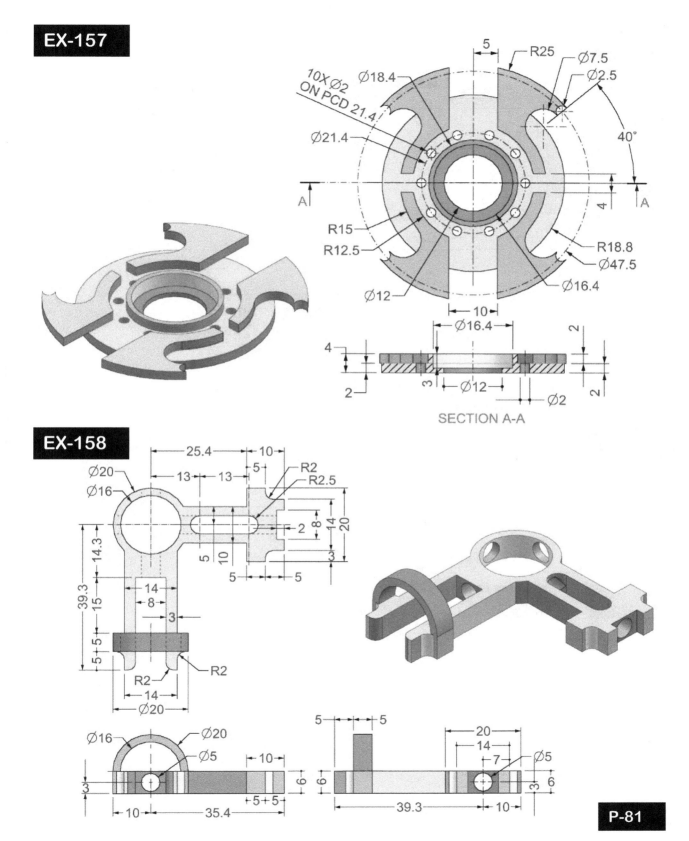

EX-157

10X Ø2 ON PCD 21.4
Ø18.4
R25
Ø7.5
Ø2.5
40°
Ø21.4
R15
R12.5
Ø12
R18.8
Ø47.5
Ø16.4
A
A
4
5

Ø16.4
10
4
2
3
Ø12
Ø2
2
2

SECTION A-A

EX-158

Ø20
Ø16
25.4
10
13
13
5
R2
R2.5
2
8
14
20
5
10
3
5
5
14.3
39.3
15
14
8
3
5
5
R2
R2
14
Ø20

Ø16
Ø20
Ø5
10
3
6
10
5 5
35.4

5
5
20
14
7
Ø5
6
6
3
39.3
10

P-81

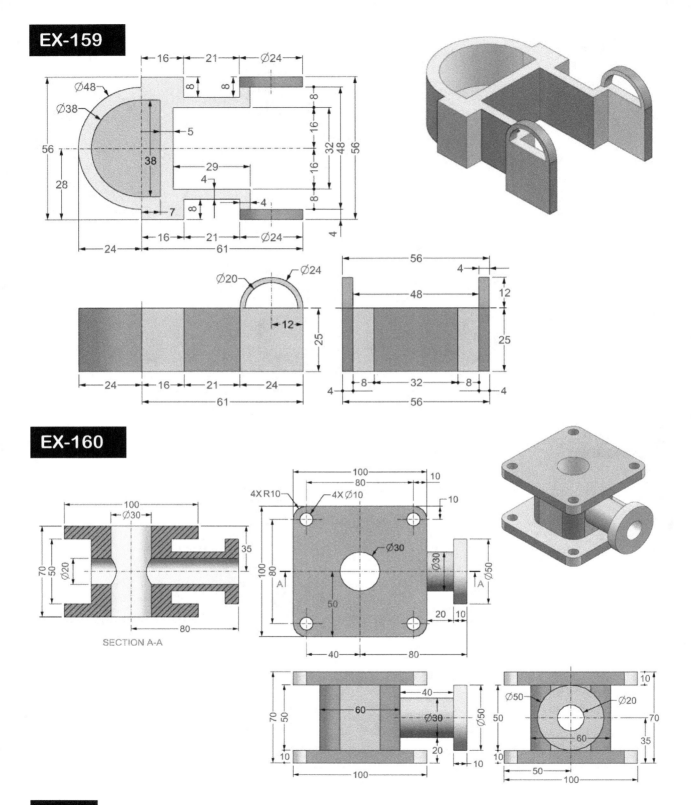

EX-159

EX-160

SECTION A-A

P-82

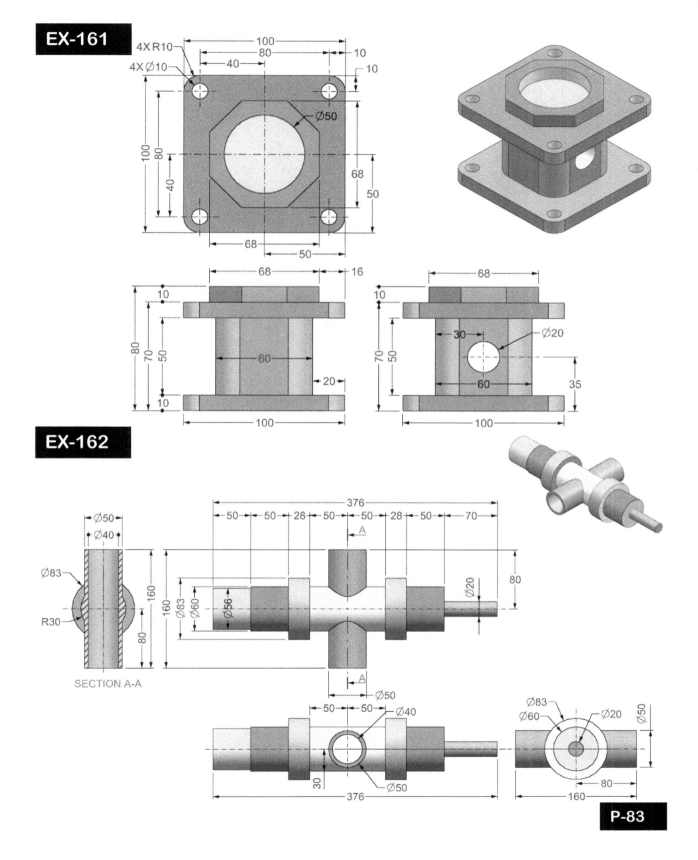

EX-161

4X R10
4X Ø10
100
80
40
10
10
Ø50
100
80
40
68
50
68
50

68
16
10
80
70
50
60
10
20
100

68
10
70
50
30
Ø20
60
35
100

EX-162

Ø50
Ø40
Ø83
R30
160
160
80

SECTION A-A

376
50 50 28 50 50 28 50 70
A
Ø83
Ø60
Ø56
80
Ø20
A
Ø50

50 50
Ø40
30
Ø50
376

Ø83
Ø60
Ø20
Ø50
80
160

P-83

EX-163

10

Ø20

SECTION A-A

20
10
Ø20
Ø20

PCD Ø160
4X Ø20
2X Ø20
2X R10
Ø20
PCD Ø80.5
Ø120

R100
Ø40

2X Ø14 THRU HOLES

TOP VIEW

SECTION B-B

10
20
Ø10

BOTTOM VIEW

Ø20
Ø40

SECTION C-C

10
Ø20
Ø20
Ø20
20

EX-164

68
28.2
4X Ø10
4X R10

10
Ø50
Ø30

68
28.2
80
100
40
A
A

10
40
40
10
80
100

16
68
16
28.2

10
10
80
70
50
25
10

Ø18

30
60
35

50
100

100
68
Ø50
10

110 110

50
25
10

Ø18

Ø30

50
50
100

SECTION A-A

P-84

EX-165

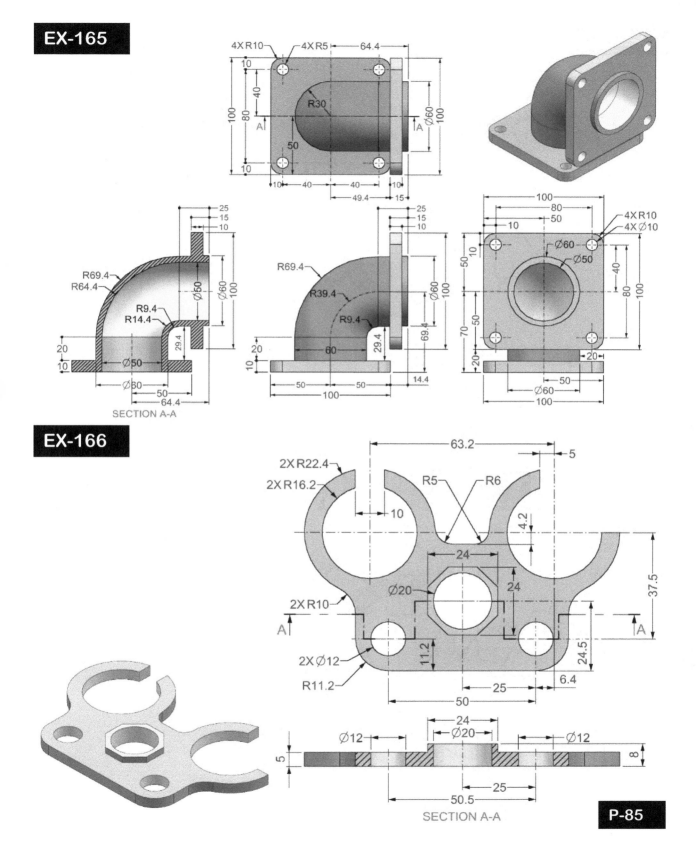

SECTION A-A

EX-166

SECTION A-A

P-85

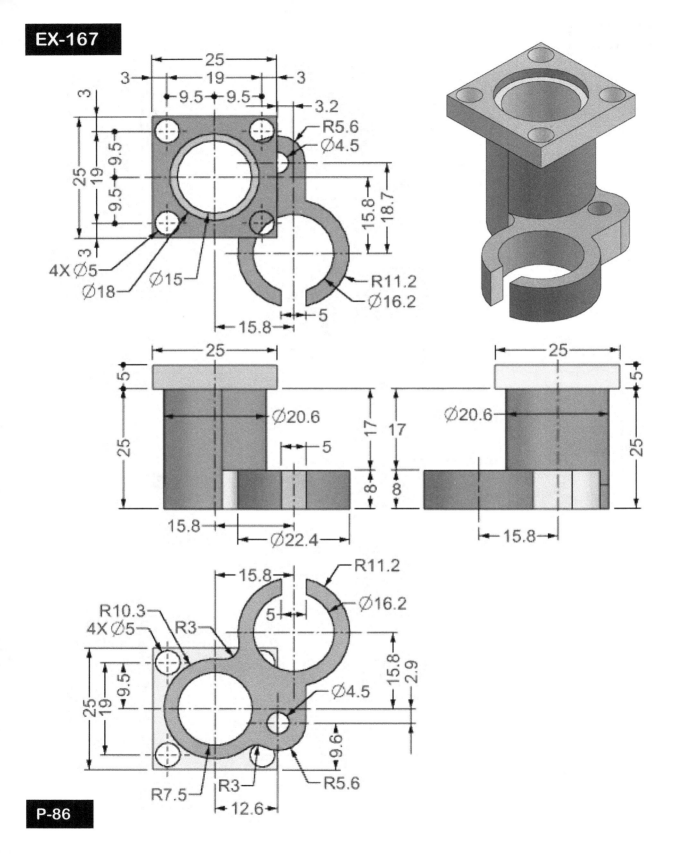

EX-167

P-86

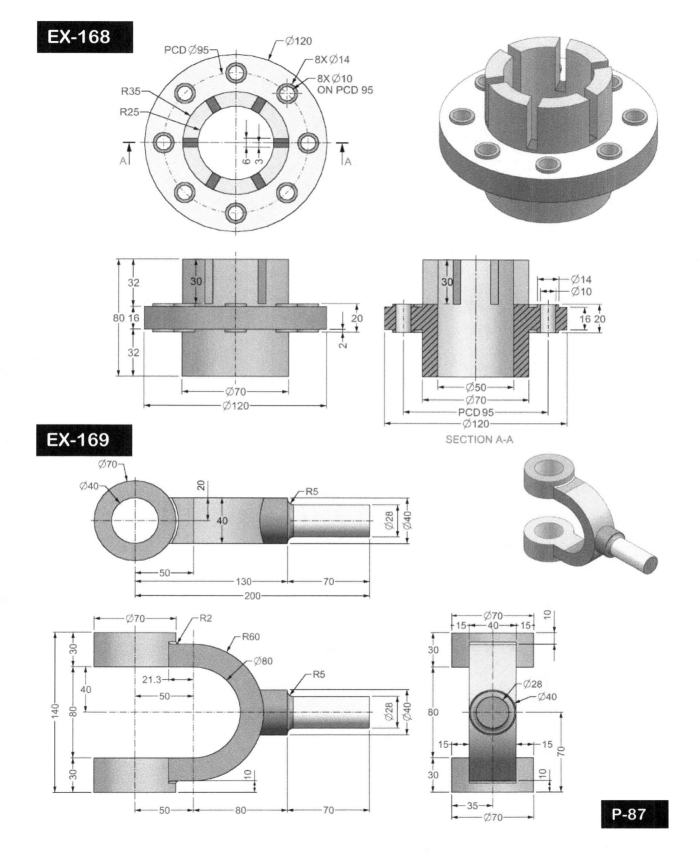

EX-168

PCD Ø95
Ø120
8X Ø14
8X Ø10
ON PCD 95
R35
R25

A
A
6
3

32
30
80 16
32
20
2

Ø70
Ø120

30
Ø14
Ø10
16 20

Ø50
Ø70
PCD 95
Ø120

SECTION A-A

EX-169

Ø70
Ø40
20
R5
40
Ø28
Ø40

50
130
70
200

Ø70
R2
R60
Ø80
R5

30
21.3
40
50
80
Ø28
Ø40
140

30
10
50
80
70

Ø70
15 40 15
10
30
Ø28
Ø40
80
70
15 15
30
35
Ø70

P-87

4X R2
3
2X Ø3
2.75
4.75
Ø15
4.75
2.75
30
1
1
1
4
6

R7.5
R6.5
R2
8.5
13
R2
8.5
8.5
15
30

1
1
7.5
4
16
1
8.5
6

44
184
44
22
92
22
4X Ø23.2
R60
40
138.6
30
30
248
168
138.6
30
30
30-20
30
124
80
40
228
272

44
20
40
44
40
264
272
20
35
40

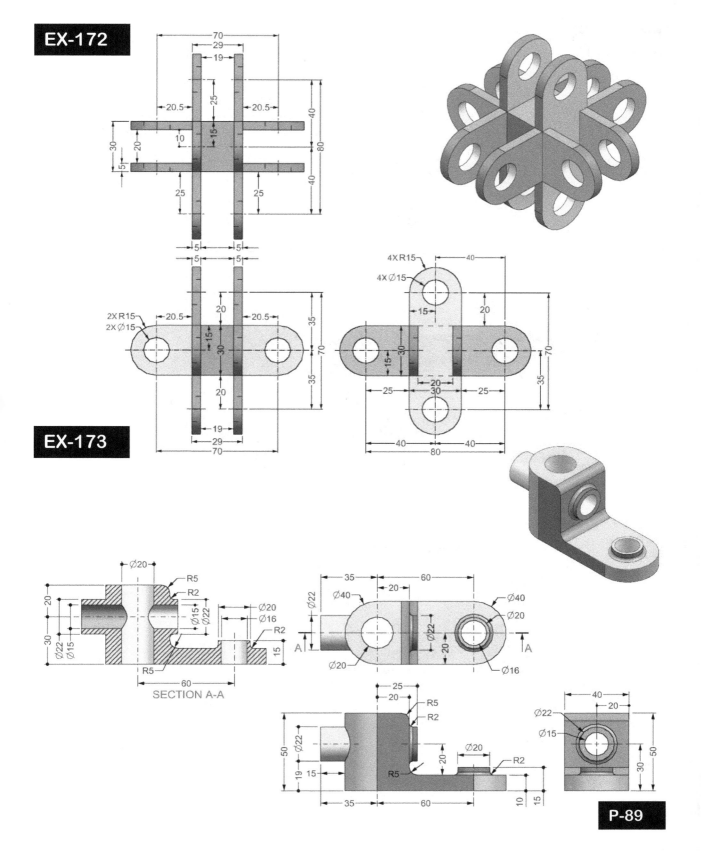

EX-172

EX-173

SECTION A-A

P-89

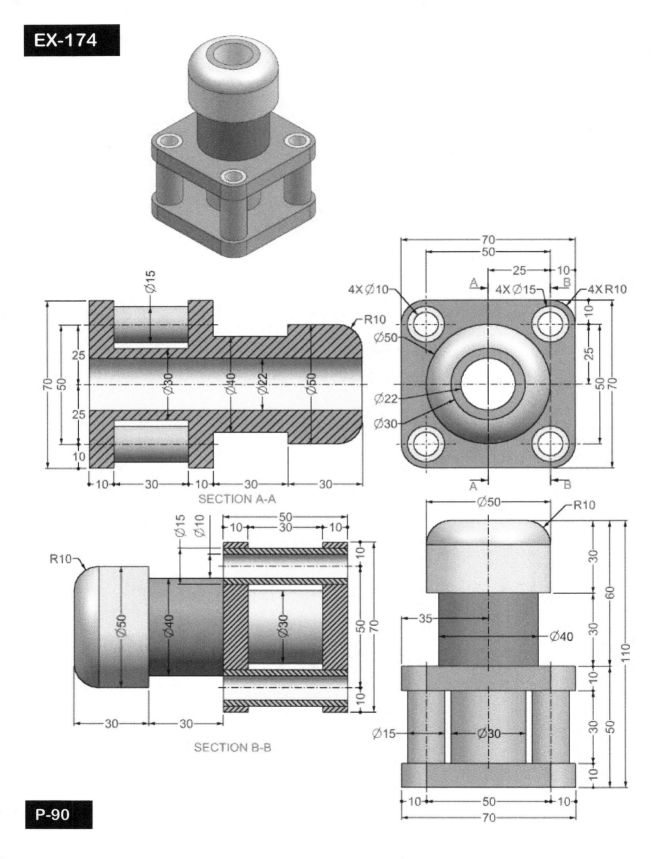

Ø15

R10

25

70
50

25

10

Ø30
Ø40
Ø22
Ø50

10   30   10   30   30

SECTION A-A

70
50
25
10

4X Ø10
A   4X Ø15   B   4X R10

R10

Ø50

Ø22

Ø30

10
25
50
70

A   B

Ø15
Ø10

R10

50
10   30   10

Ø50
Ø40

Ø30

10
70
50
10

30   30

SECTION B-B

Ø50   R10

30
60

35   Ø40

30

10

Ø15   Ø30

30
110
50

10

10   50   10
70

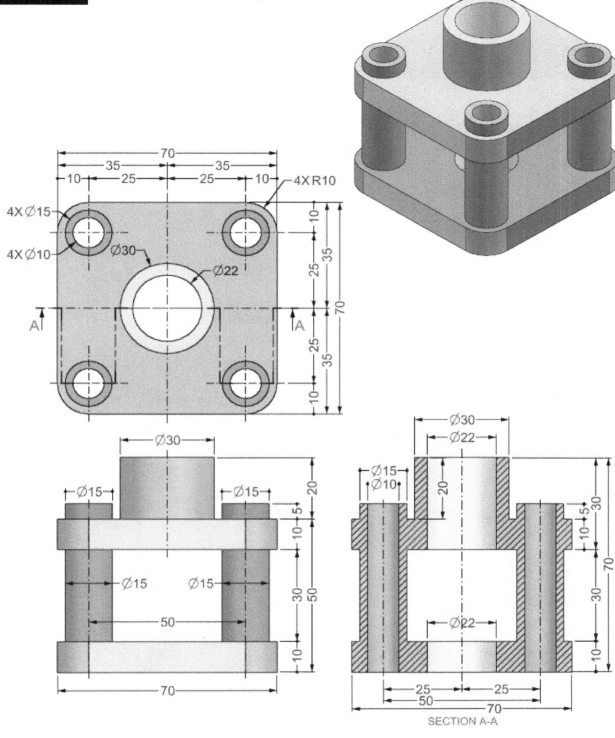

SECTION A-A

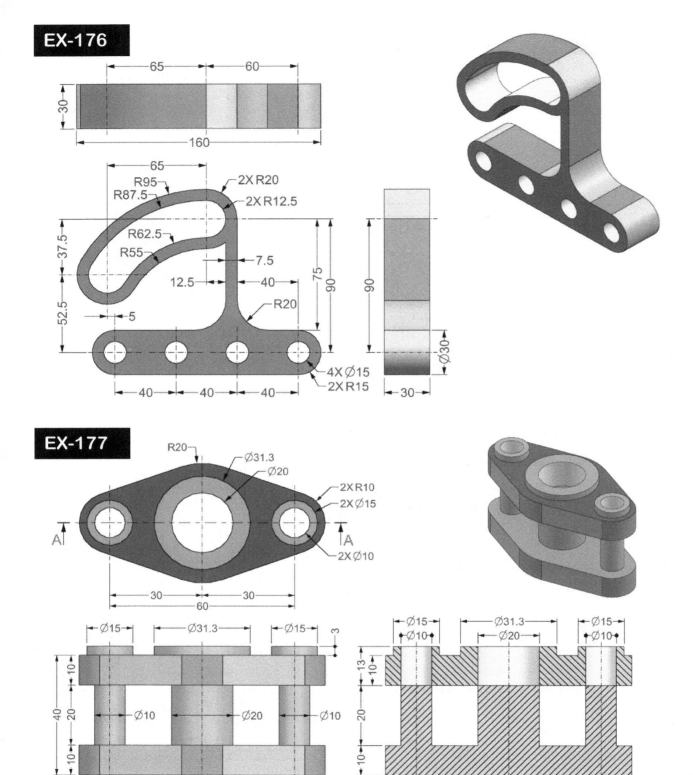

EX-176

65
60
30
160

65
R95
R87.5
2X R20
2X R12.5
R62.5
R55
37.5
52.5
7.5
12.5
40
5
R20
75
90
90
∅30
30

40
40
40
4X ∅15
2X R15

EX-177

R20
∅31.3
∅20
2X R10
2X ∅15
2X ∅10
A
A

30
30
60

∅15
∅31.3
∅15
3
∅10
∅20
∅10
40
20
10
10

30
30
60

∅15
∅31.3
∅15
∅10
∅20
∅10
13
10
20
10

30
30
60
SECTION A-A

P-92

EX-178

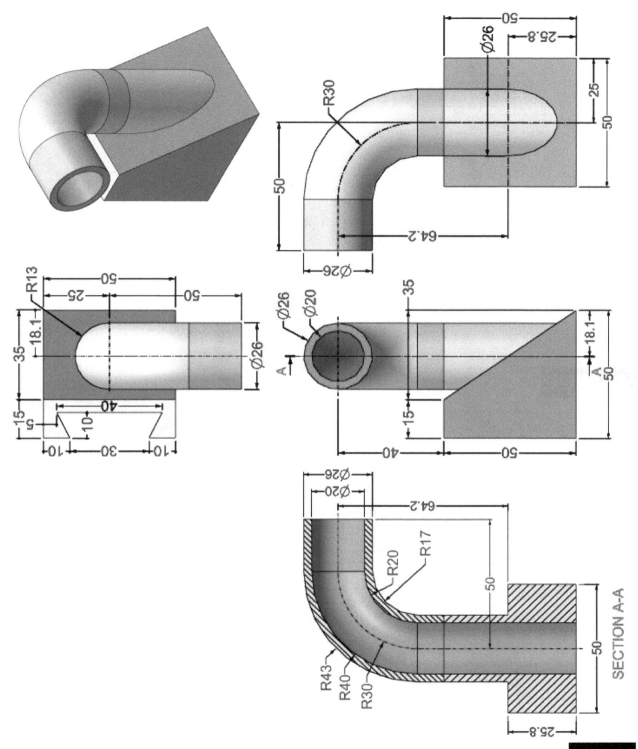

SECTION A-A

P-93

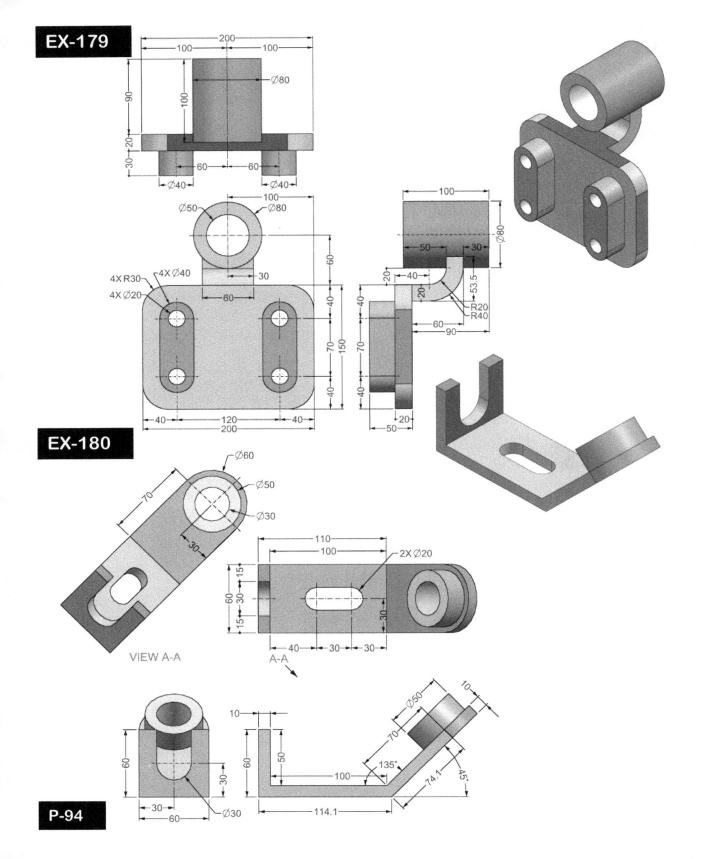

EX-179

200
100 100
Ø80
90
100
20
30
60 60
Ø40 Ø40

Ø50 100 Ø80
4X R30 4X Ø40
4X Ø20
30
60
60
40
150
70
40
40 120 40
200

100
50 30
Ø80
20
40
20
70
40
R20
R40
60
90
20
50

EX-180

Ø60
70 Ø50
Ø30
30

110
100 2X Ø20
15
60 30
15 30
40 30 30

VIEW A-A   A-A

P-94

60
30
30
30
60 Ø30

10
60 50
100
135°
Ø50
70
10
74.1
45°
114.1

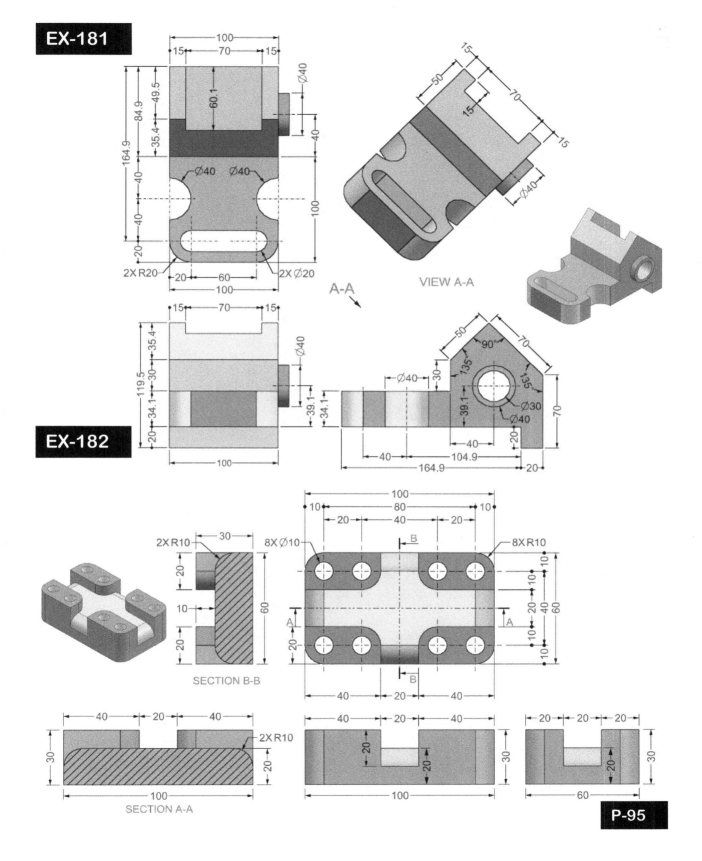

EX-181

EX-182

VIEW A-A

A-A

SECTION B-B

SECTION A-A

P-95

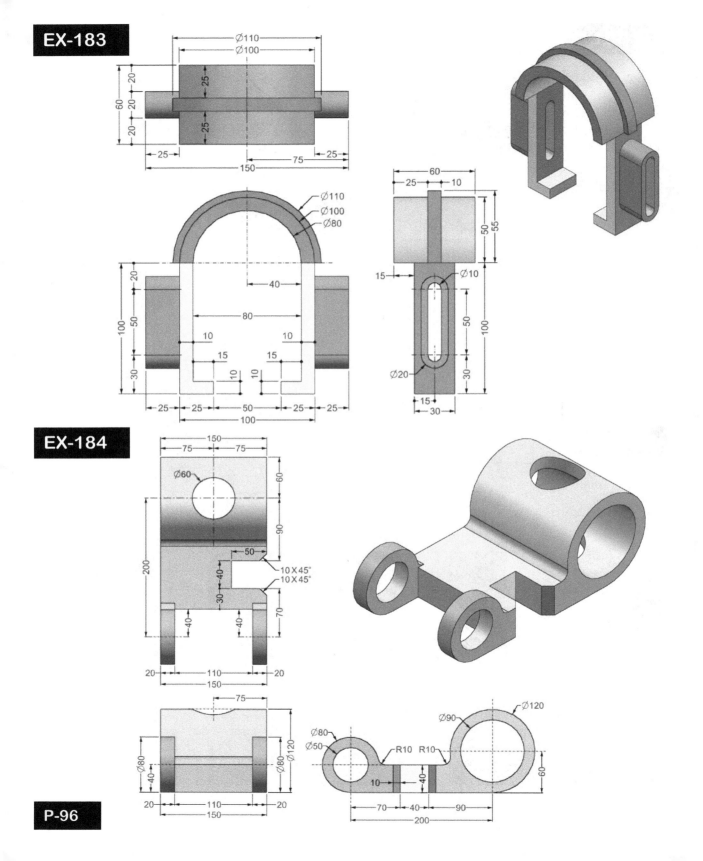

EX-183

Ø110
Ø100
60
20
20
20
25
25
25
75
25
150

Ø110
Ø100
Ø80
20
100
50
30
40
80
10   10
15   15
10   10
25   25   50   25   25
100

60
25   10
50
55
15   Ø10
50
100
Ø20   30
15
30

EX-184

150
75   75
Ø60
60
90
200
50
10 X 45°
40
10 X 45°
30
70
40   40
20   110   20
150

75
Ø80
Ø80
Ø120
40
20   110   20
150

Ø120
Ø80
Ø90
Ø50
R10 R10
10   40
60
70   40   90
200

P-96

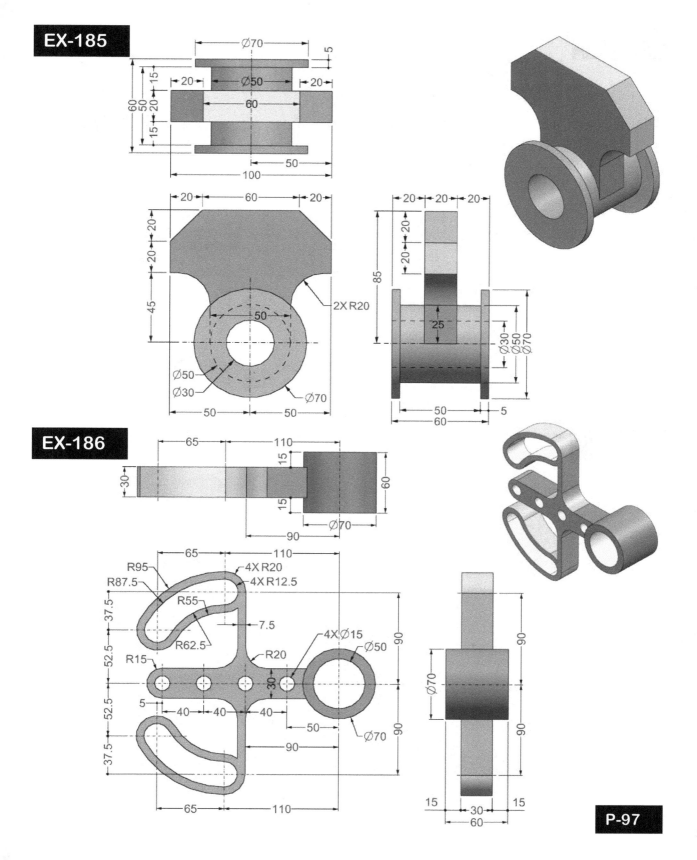

EX-185

Ø70
5
15
20
Ø50
60
60
50
20
15
20
100
50

20
60
20
20
20
45
2X R20
50
Ø50
Ø30
Ø70
50
50

20
20
20
85
20
20
20
25
Ø30
Ø50
Ø70
50
5
60

EX-186

65
110
15
30
60
15
Ø70
90

65
110
R95
4X R20
R87.5
4X R12.5
R55
37.5
7.5
R62.5
52.5
4X Ø15
R15
R20
Ø50
30
5
40
40
40
52.5
50
Ø70
90
37.5
65
110

90
Ø70
90
15
30
15
60

P-97

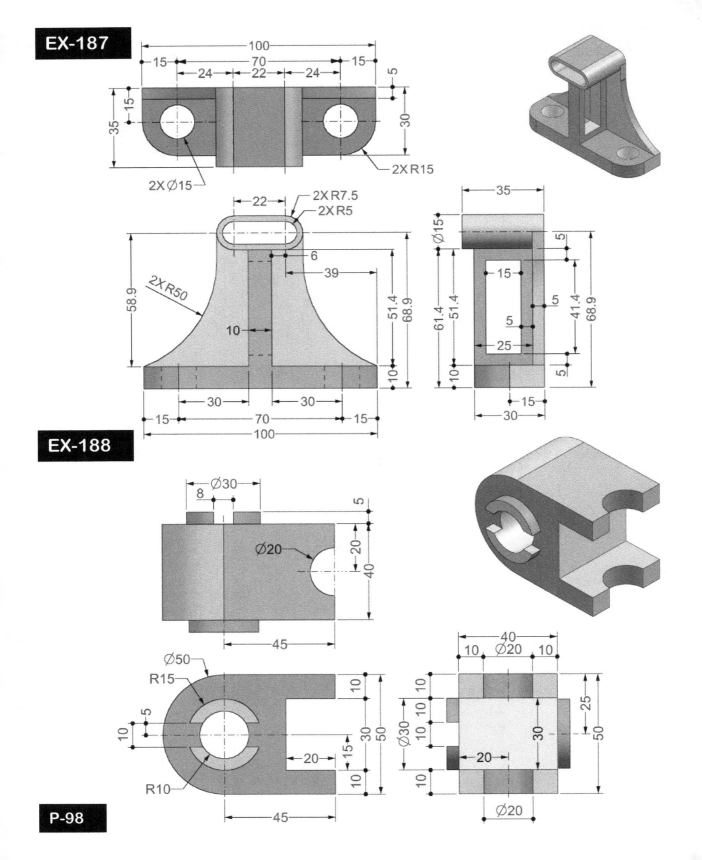

EX-187

100
15 70 15
24 22 24
5
15
35 30
2X R15
2X Ø15

2X R7.5
2X R5
22
58.9
2X R50
6
39
10
51.4
68.9
10
30 30
15 70 15
100

35
Ø15
5
15
5
61.4
51.4
41.4
68.9
5
10
25
5
15
30

EX-188

Ø30
8
5
Ø20
20
40
45

Ø50
R15
10
5
10
30
50
20
15
R10
10
45

40
10 Ø20 10
10
Ø30 10
10
10
25
30
50
20
10
Ø20

P-98

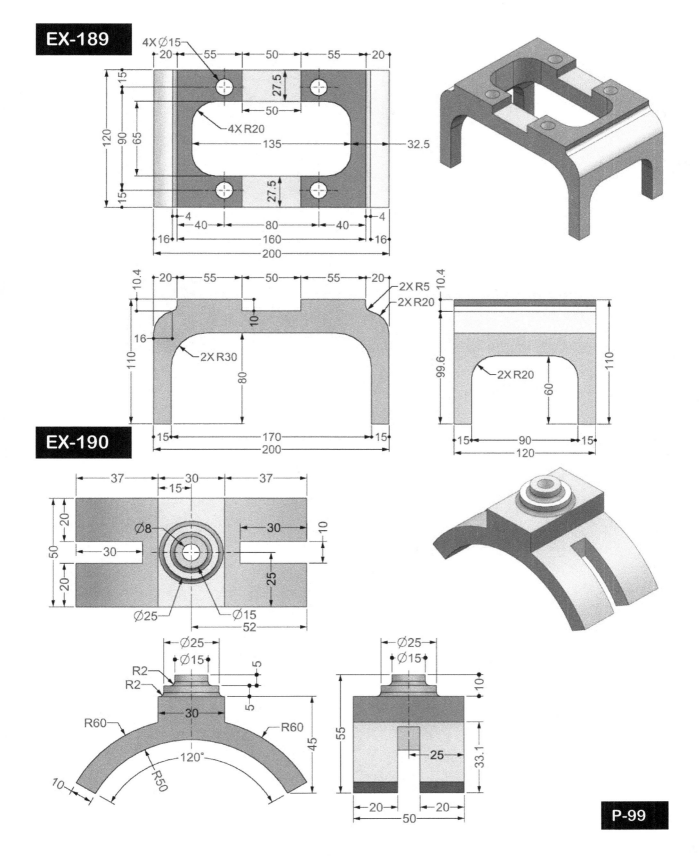

EX-189

4X Ø15
20 · 55 · 50 · 55 · 20
15
120
90
65
27.5
50
4X R20
135
32.5
15
27.5
4
40
80
40
4
16
160
16
200

20 · 55 · 50 · 55 · 20
10.4
2X R5
2X R20
16
110
2X R30
80
10
15 · 170 · 15
200

EX-190

10.4
99.6
2X R20
60
110
15 · 90 · 15
120

37 · 30 · 37
15
20
50
20
Ø8
30
30
10
25
Ø25 · Ø15
52

Ø25
Ø15
R2
R2
5
5
R60
30
R60
45
120°
R50
10

Ø25
Ø15
10
55
33.1
25
20 · 20
50

P-99

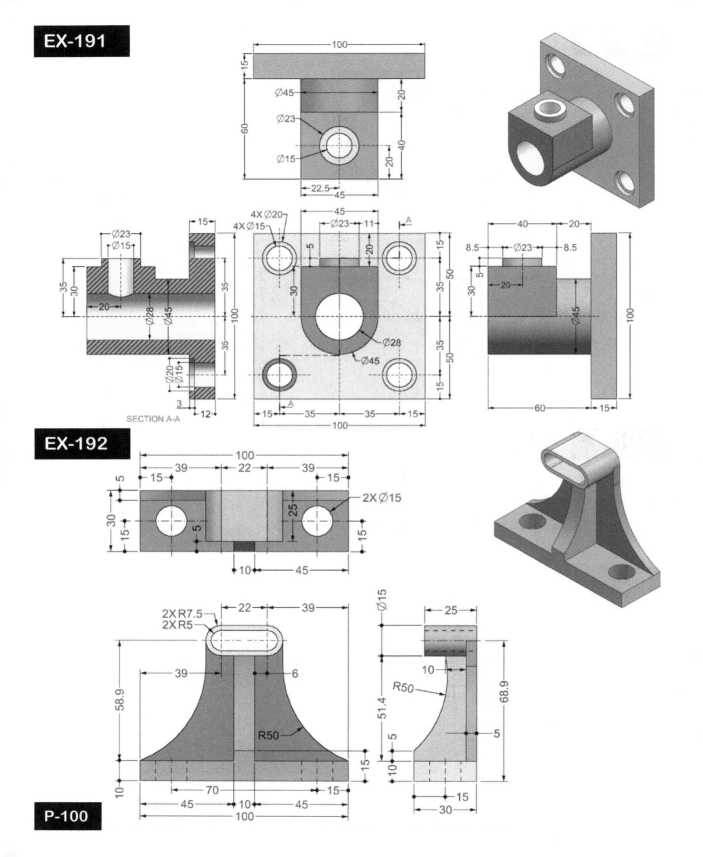

EX-191

EX-192

P-100

EX-193

SECTION A-A

40
12
10
10
80
60
R2
Ø20
Ø30
1 x 45°
30
10
Ø8
Ø14

Ø30
15
Ø30
40
2X Ø14
2X R10
2X Ø8
R20
30
60
30
10
Ø20
Ø30
55
A
A

Ø30
Ø23
15
R2
R2
55
Ø30
Ø14
40
12
10

40
Ø30
Ø14
20
R3.2
40
10
12
30
30
60

EX-194

150
4X Ø20
20
110
20
55
20
40
40
15
R5
15
130
30
60
40
30
Ø120
40
70
35
40

ALL HOLES CHAMFER 2MM

130°
2X Ø20
2X Ø50
Ø120
25°
R5
PCD Ø160
Ø100
75
80
R5
40
R5
40
70
40
35

60
30
15
80
30
40
20
R5
40
130

70
50
60
4X Ø20
20
20
110
150
BOTTOM VIEW

P-101

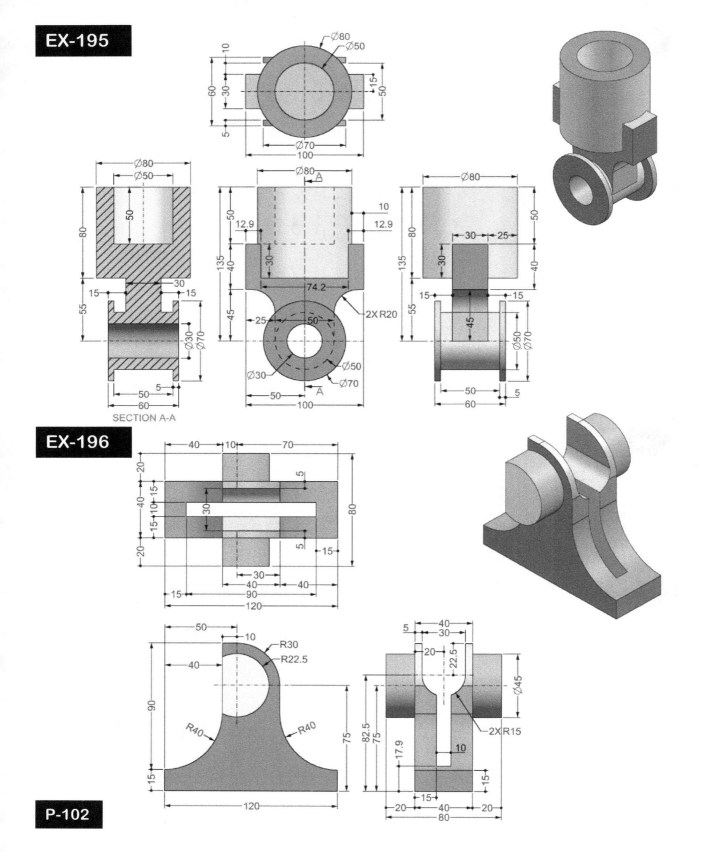

EX-195

Ø80
Ø50
10
60
30
15
50
5
Ø70
100

Ø80
Ø50
50
80
15
30
15
55
Ø30
Ø70
50
5
60
SECTION A-A

Ø80
A
50
10
12.9
12.9
135
50
40
30
74.2
45
25
50
2X R20
Ø30
50
Ø50
Ø70
A
50
100

Ø80
50
80
30
25
135
30
15
15
55
45
Ø50
Ø70
50
5
60

EX-196

40
10
70
20
5
40
15
10
15
30
15
80
5
15
20
30
40
40
90
15
120

50
10
R30
R22.5
40
90
R40
R40
75
15
120

5
40
30
20
22.5
82.5
Ø45
75
17.9
10
2X R15
15
15
20
40
20
80

P-102

EX-197

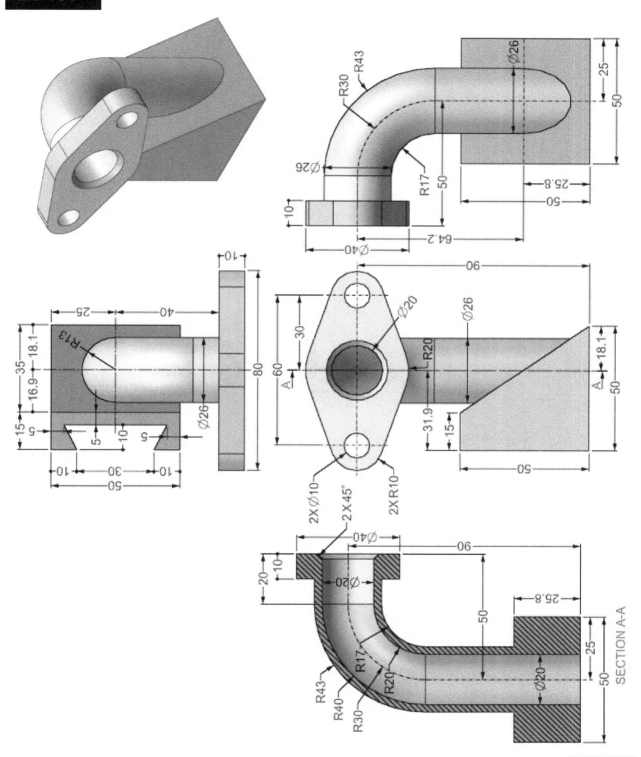

SECTION A-A

P-103

6X Ø15THRU
ON PCD 90
Ø120
Ø50
Ø40
PCD Ø90

A   A

VIEW B-B

8X Ø10THRU
ON PCD 54
Ø30
Ø70
Ø20
PCD Ø54

Ø120
Ø50
Ø40
15
10
Ø15
120
30
B-B
5
10
60°
60°
Ø20
Ø30 54
PCD 54
80
Ø10

SECTION A-A

EX-199

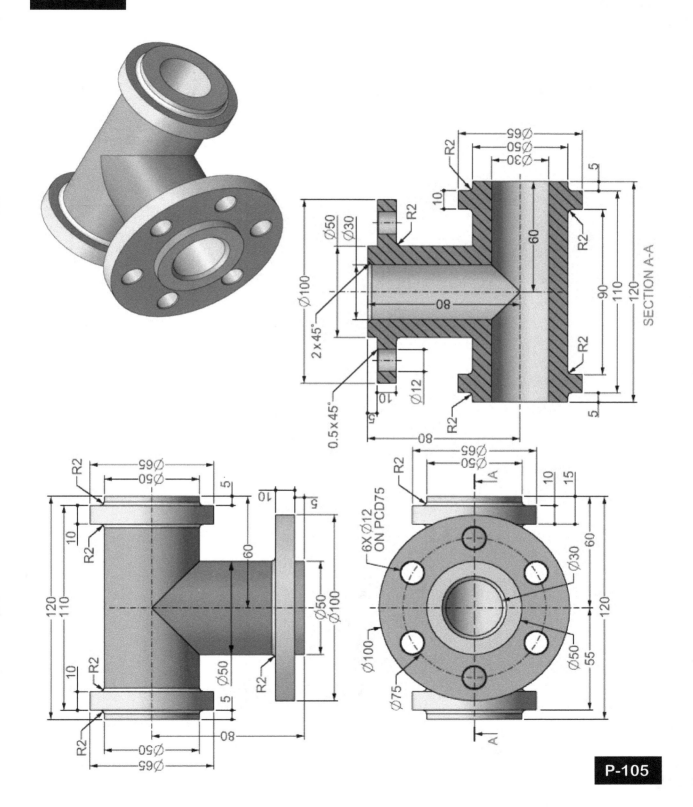

SECTION A-A

6X⌀12
ON PCD75

P-105

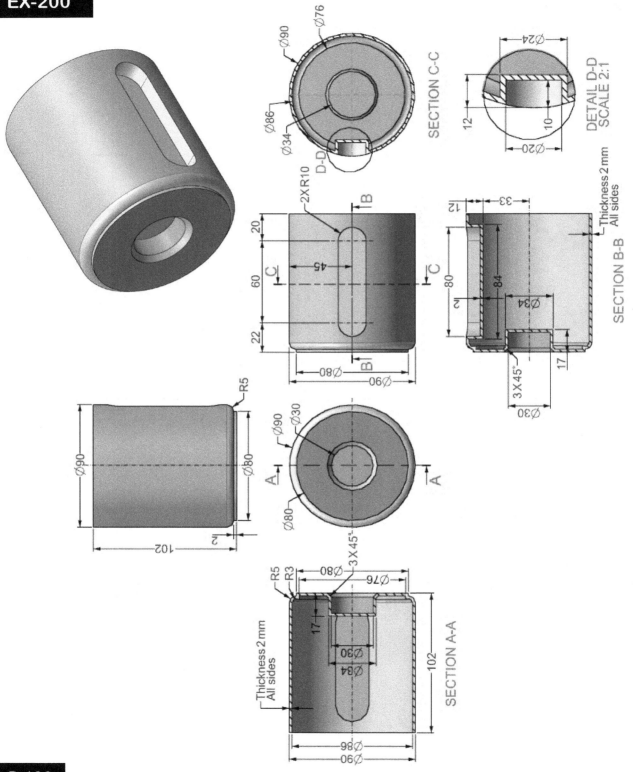

2X R10

SECTION C-C

Ø90
Ø76
Ø86
Ø34
D-D

DETAIL D-D
SCALE 2:1

Ø24
12
10
Ø20

Thickness 2 mm
All sides

SECTION B-B

33
12
80
Ø34
3 X 45°
17
Ø30

20
60
22
45
Ø80
Ø90
B
C
C
B

R5
Ø90
Ø80
102
2

Ø90
Ø30
Ø80
A
A

SECTION A-A

R5
R3
3 X 45°
Ø80
Ø76
17
Ø30
Ø84
Thickness 2 mm
All sides
Ø86
Ø90
102

Other useful books by CADIN360

1. 150 CAD Exercises

2. AutoCAD Exercises

3. CAD Exercises

4. 50+ SolidWorks Exercises

5. SolidWorks 200 Exercises

6. Autodesk Inventor Exercises

7. Catia Exercises

8. Siemens NX Exercises

www.ingramcontent.com/pod-product-compliance
Lightning Source LLC
Chambersburg PA
CBHW060447060326
40689CB00020B/4462